WINNING WITH...MORTGAGE FINANCE

Home Mortgage Finance Guide

Copyright ©2004
Revised 2013

Library of Congress -in-Publication Data
March 2004
Winning With Mortgage Finance

10 9 8 7 6 5 4 3 2 1

The enclosed material is designed for educational purposes only. Each State may have different certification and specific guidelines. Please refer to your State for additional and future information. The information contained herein is considered correct at the time of creation but laws and regulations are updated frequently and the reader assumes the responsibility for confirming current regulations and applicable data. The publisher and author make no warranty as to the success of the individuals using the training material contained herein. The publisher and author make no warranty as to any action taken by any individual completing this program. The reader is responsible for the appropriate use of the materials and information provided. This publication is designed to provide accurate and authoritative information concerning the subject matter. All material is sold with the understanding that neither the author nor the publisher guarantees the actions of any individual making use of the inclusions. Neither the author nor the publisher is rendering a legal opinion, accounting recommendation or other professional service. If legal advice or other expert assistance is desired, the services of a legal professional or other individual should be sought. The applicable federally released forms, disclosures and notices are generated from public domain. Copyright law does apply to all intellectual materials and all rights under said law are reserved b y the copyright owner.

Coursework is available at special quantity discounts to use as premiums and sales promotions within corporate or private training programs. To obtain information or inquire about availability please write to Director, PO Box 1, Hollidaysburg, PA 16648.

NOTICE

WINNING WITH...MORTGAGE FINANCE

Home Mortgage Finance Guide

I

Introduction

A mortgage is the dream financial transaction. Someone will give you the money that you need to buy the home of your dreams and all you really need to provide is your signature on a few documents. Right?

You begin the process full of energy, enthusiasm, and excitement. You are making the biggest purchase of your life, fulfilling the American Dream and you just cannot help but be excited as you work diligently with your Real Estate Agent. With a sense of anticipation, you set out to search for the perfect home. This home will be the one that you can afford, the seller wants to sell to you, and will fulfill the dream of stability for you and your family.

You search the MLS service listings provided by your agent. You wander through dozens of houses while you try to locate the perfect home for you and your family. Finally, one day, you realize that you have found it. The search is finally over and you are ready to move onto the next chapter in your life.

All that is left to do is make an offer that the seller will find acceptable, get your mortgage, and pick up the keys to your new dream home. From here, the process is smooth and simple.

You make an offer on the home that the seller's accept. The only condition that you can see on the seller's acceptance of your offer is that you must be pre-approved by a lender within 10 days from the date of acceptance.

All you need to do now is find yourself a good home lender who will provide the money that you need so that you can finish this process and move into your new home. Most Real Estate Agents will provide you with three referral names that you can contact to get your mortgage funds. They provide three so that you will have the opportunity to choose the lender and loan officer that is right for you and your transaction.

At this point, the sense of anticipation will be high. You have successfully located the home of your dreams. You are a few days or perhaps weeks from moving into that home. You open the telephone book and discover that choosing a lender, even to decide which of the referral lenders the Realtor gave you might be a bit more daunting than you expected. The yellow pages have lenders and brokers. There are loans to purchase, cash-out your equity, and refinance your loan, even loans to buy and restore a home. The lists appear to go on forever and, unfortunately, there is no glossary of terms in the back of the telephone book. So you should just pick one and get the ball rolling, right?

Well, let's consider. You have expended a great deal of energy choosing the perfect home. You and your family are already dreaming about all of the fun that you will have once you move into your new house. You are getting ready to spend more money on a single purchase than you have probably spent in your lifetime. Your sales agreement clearly states that the only major obstacle between you and the closing table is obtaining a loan. You have heard that the home loan process requires you to pay fees and you do not want to spend more than you need to get financing. You know you will need to provide documentation and sign tons of paperwork in order to get the lender to give the seller the money you have promised but are not sure exactly what you need to bring to the lender. The telephone books advertisements alone show hundreds of different types of loans and offer funding for many different types of borrowers. You have no idea what type of borrower you are or even what type of loan you need.

Essentially, although you have located and successfully made an acceptable offer for the home you want, the process is far from complete. There is still a great deal left for you to do before you can get your hands on the keys to that new house.

So what do you do? Take what you have learned on the street, cross your fingers and just call a lender? Put all of your faith and money in the hands of an employee from the lender's office and hope for the best? These options could prove costly for you and your family. The only safe option is to become better informed.

Lending appears to be a complicated process, but with a few simple tools, some knowledge, and a lot of preparation you can make it very simple. By being better informed you will be able to better negotiate your loan and save yourself hundreds or even thousands of dollars in up-front closing costs and interest payments over the life of your loan.

When choosing a company and individual to aid you with your home financing needs it is important to remember that your loan process and products will only be as good as the employee you hire. You will want to retain the services of a person who is able to handle your loan professionally, cost-effectively, and quickly. The loan officer that you hire should also be able to add the creativity required customizing the loan products that are available to suit your particular situation rather than just placing you in the most common or most familiar loan product. A loan officer who will spend a few extra minutes thinking about the loan products that are available to suit your particular situation can save you tremendous amounts of money over the life of your loan.

Before you begin searching for the loan officer that will suit you the best in your loan process, you will need to understand the different employment environments in which they may work. There are two primary employers for loan officers. The act of choosing the correct forum can, and often does, have a dramatic impact on the loan product that you receive and the amount of money that you spend over the life of your loan. Using the correct lender can make your processes smooth, efficient and save you a great deal of money.

This book is designed to assist you in gaining all of the knowledge you need to complete all of the mortgage processes necessary to reach loan funding and to provide you with an incredible edge in any mortgage negotiation process.

Who will work hardest for me?
Choosing a Lender

The first decision you will make before ever picking up the telephone to call a lender is what type of lender you want to work for you. The two primary options are the mortgage bank and the mortgage brokerage. When you looked in the telephone book, you saw both of these designations but did not really consider the differences implied by the names. You might ask if the type of lender that you choose can really make any difference to you if the result is that you get the money you need to buy your house. The answer is a resounding yes!

The mortgage market is divided into two classifications.

- The primary mortgage market

- The secondary mortgage market

The primary mortgage market is the area where lenders work directly with borrowers to originate, document and close loans. Examples of entities within the primary mortgage market are:

- Mortgage Brokerage Offices
- Savings Banks
- Commercial Banks
- Mutual Savings Banks
- Credit Unions

These lending institutions work directly with borrowers who need funding to purchase real estate.

The employees who work within the mortgage department at these locations are loan processors, loan originators, mortgage brokers, and loan officers.

COMMON TITLES

A **Loan Originator** is someone who spends a great part of the workday on the streets soliciting borrower referrals from affinity groups. They bring these borrower referrals back to their office, structure the loan package that meets the borrowers needs, and document a package that will enable the lending institution to fund a solid loan.

A **Loan Officer** is someone who spends a great deal of his or her time in the office, interviewing potential borrowers and structuring the available loan products to meet the needs and specific situation of the borrower. The primary goal of the loan officer is to ensure that each loan closed provides all of the parties involved with the best possible loan package.

A **Mortgage Broker** is someone who uses their vast knowledge of the mortgage industry to bring potential borrower packages to the right lending institution and obtain the loan program that meets the needs of both the borrower and lender. The broker acts as a liaison bringing the potential borrowers together with the right lender and loan program to ensure that the borrower achieves their dreams of homeownership.

A **Loan Processor** assists the borrower in obtaining all of the documents and services that are required to complete the loan process and purchase transaction. The essential element of the loan-processing career is to act as a liaison between the borrower and all other individuals whose assistance is required to achieve a closed loan. The loan processor's primary focus during the loan process is to complete all of the necessary tasks in a timely manner and to ensure that all items incorporated into the closing package are correct and free of errors.

Each of these individuals will work directly with you to accomplish the tasks that lead to a home loan funding.

- Complete the mortgage loan application or 1003.

- Obtain loan stipulations or documentation required by the stipulations list or sales agreement.

- Order affiliate services such as Title Searches and Appraisals.

- Generate the good faith estimate.

- Provide all required disclosures and notifications to you.

- Structure the mortgage loan funding and down payment to meet the parameters of the loan approval.

- Arrange and oversee your closing on the property.

Many borrowers assume that the bank where they make the loan application funds the mortgage loans through available cash resulting from the deposits of the individuals who conduct their banking activity at that bank. In some cases, this is exactly where the funds required to provide a mortgage loan originate. However, these depository funds are often inadequate to meet the borrowing needs of all of the individuals who obtain loan proceeds from the local institution.

SECONDARY MORTGAGE MARKET

Lenders within the primary mortgage market will underwrite and fund mortgage loans that the borrower applies for with the cash that they have on hand. Once the lender has a group of funded loan packages, they will combine the many funded loan packages into one large package and offer it for sale to the secondary mortgage market.

The secondary mortgage market includes entities such as

- Insurance Companies
- Primary Lenders with excess deposits
- Pension Funds
- Individual Investors

The secondary mortgage market purchases funded and closed loans from the direct lender in the primary mortgage market.

- This purchase of the closed loans enables the banks and institutions within the primary market to fund more loans than would be possible if they had to fund and service all of the debt load within their portfolio themselves.

- This funding enables the entities on the secondary market to obtain the return on their investment generated through the interest and penalty figures applied to the borrowed funds.

-

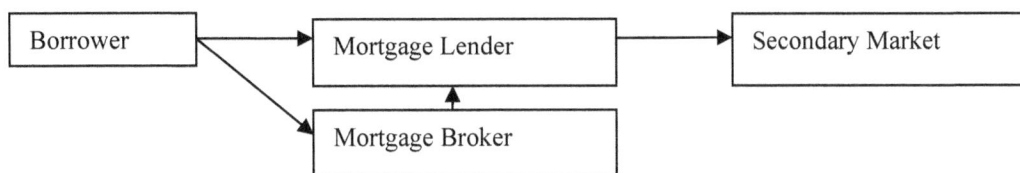

Figure 1:1 Mortgage Market Structure

The borrower makes a mortgage application with a mortgage loan officer or mortgage loan processor who works in a mortgage bank or mortgage brokerage. A mortgage bank usually funds its own loans while a mortgage brokerage does not lend its own money. A brokerage works with multiple funding sources to find the correct lender for each borrower.

The mortgage bank or loan funding institution then packages the loan with other loans that have been funded with their capital.

- If the overall loan package is large enough (worth enough money), the funding institution offers that package for sale to investors within the secondary mortgage market.

- If the mortgage-funding source does not have enough loan products to package into large enough groups to meet the needs of the secondary mortgage market, they will package them into smaller groups and offer the package to another lending institution or a smaller investing group.

This smaller group of investors forms what is termed an investing pool. An investing pool can include anyone who is seeking a low risk, long-term investment and has the capital available to purchase the packaged loan products.

This investing pool will then collect the interest on the loans that they have purchased and achieve the return on their capital investment that meets their needs.

- If the loans are packaged and sold to another lending institution, that institution will package the purchased loans with their own funded loan packages and create an overall offering large enough for the secondary mortgage market.

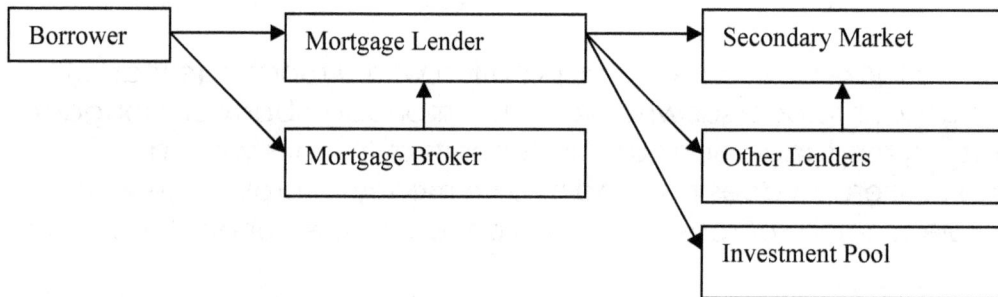

```
┌──────────┐        ┌─────────────────┐        ┌─────────────────┐
│ Borrower │──────▶ │ Mortgage Lender │──────▶ │ Secondary Market│
└──────────┘    ▲   └─────────────────┘        └─────────────────┘
           ╲    │            ▲                          ▲
            ╲   │            │                          │
        ┌─────────────────┐  │        ┌─────────────────┐
        │ Mortgage Broker │──┘        │  Other Lenders  │
        └─────────────────┘           └─────────────────┘

                                      ┌─────────────────┐
                                      │ Investment Pool │
                                      └─────────────────┘
```

Figure 1:2 Expanded Mortgage Market Structure

The Mortgage Bank

A bank is a lending institution that typically funds loans using their own money. The benefits of working with a "bank" are obvious.

- Traditional banking institutions are typically located within the community that they serve. This means that you can walk right in and talk to your loan officer and that the bank is likely one that you or someone that you know has worked with in the past.

- Traditional lenders often retain their own team of loan underwriters, processors, closers, and post-closers that will enable you to create a "team" atmosphere that may assist in smoother loan processes and closings. Your goals with your team will be the same – a good loan, smooth processes, and satisfying results. In addition, these loans are usually funded in house so once you get an approval there are typically no changes to the loan terms.

Working with a bank also has its downside.

- A bank will usually have specific qualifying guidelines and limited products available. If you do not fit within those guidelines or qualify for those products then your loan application will be declined. No matter how much you like that bank or loan officer, you will need to "shop" other lenders if you want a loan.

The Mortgage Broker

A mortgage broker acts as a liaison between the borrower and the funding source. They typically do not fund any loans of their own. The broker will frequently fulfill the task of shopping for the perfect loan for the borrower.

- These offices are typically less well known than banks and so you will need to research reliability and background of any broker you select.

- A broker does offer a wider variety of loan programs. You will find most brokerages have contracted to write loans for between 10 and 200 different lenders. This variety allows you to shop many programs with one application making it relatively easy for the loan officer to find programs that are just right for your situation.

- Admittedly, you are not on the same "team" as your underwriters, closers and post-closers but you will find that if you and your loan officer build a respectful rapport with these individuals your goals are the same – a closed loan.

At a brokerage, the loan officer cannot only place most loans; they will be able to come up with a variety of options for you. Rather than one cut and dry approval that may kill your deal at the time of initial underwriting review, they should be able to find options that allow them to customize the loan program to suit your needs. One lender may offer a lower interest rate but expect a rather steep down payment. If you are cash poor but willing to make a higher monthly payment the broker can look for another lender willing to charge a slightly higher rate in exchange for less money down. These variations in loan product requirements are where the creativity of the loan officer you have chosen comes into play. There are as many ways to put a loan package together as there are borrowers in your town.

Once you have made the decision regarding the type of mortgage office you wish to work with, you must make one more decision regarding the initial service provider. You must choose the loan officer who will work for you. The importance of choosing your loan officer with care cannot be emphasized enough. Do not just telephone different offices until you find a loan officer willing to quote you the best interest rate on the telephone. The loan product you end up with will undoubtedly vary greatly from the one quoted to you on the first telephone call.

Begin by asking friends, relatives, co-workers, just about anyone you know about their home buying experiences. This will help you to determine what lending office and specifically, which loan officer, is a competent and fair professional.

You should interview loan officers as you would any employee you were thinking of hiring. Many people do not think about the fact that when you retain a service provider you are actually hiring that individual as a short-term employee. As you will learn in the section regarding closing costs and fees, you will pay the loan officer well for the services that they perform on your behalf. Since you are paying the bill, you have the right to choose the loan officer you want working on your loan package.

Your interview should include a look at any "brag book" materials the loan officer may have available. The brag book should include items that tell you what credentials and training your loan officer has obtained. It should also show you how well the loan officer has performed for past customers. Some States require that a loan officer successfully complete a training program while others do not have any criteria for lending professionals. If you live in a State that has no professional education or licensure requirements, it is doubly important that you properly screen the professional you hire. Just consider, if there is no educational requirement for becoming a mortgage professional, anyone can put out a shingle and begin working in the lending arena. You will want to discuss experience and certification with the loan officer you are considering hiring. They may have achieved a certificate of completion for a lending training program. Many competent loan officers will be able to provide you with items from previous customers – letters, thank you cards, even notes, that show they performed in an efficient and professional manner. Some lenders will have received awards or certificates that show past performance successes. Each of these items will help you screen potential lending candidates and provide you with vital insight into how the loan officer has performed when working with other loan applicants.

Do not be afraid to ask the prospective loan officer questions. They are interviewing to perform a service for you. As such, they should competently answer any questions you choose to put to them. Later we will review some sample questions you may wish to use.

The last important factor to consider when choosing a loan officer is personality. You will want to choose a lending representative whose work style matches your needs. If you are a numbers person who prefers to have the bare bones facts, you will not want to choose a lender who has based their career on social skills. Conversely, if you are the type of person who feels most comfortable negotiating a deal in a relaxed, conversational manner, you will not want to choose a lending representative who is a by the book and to the point loan officer.

Before setting your first appointment with a loan officer, you should spend some time planning your purchase strategy as well as your budget and loan product preferences. You will need to revise these items once you have chosen your lender. Having an idea of your wants and needs at the time of interview allows the loan officer to see how informed and committed you are to your purchase. Being fully informed also allows the lender to assess your knowledge and needs with an eye toward planning your loan programs.

The last item you should have available for your interview process is a list of questions.

Questions serve a purpose beyond showing preparation and interest. Many people fear the loan application process. They become nervous and tongue-tied. This occurs with good reason. When you walk into an application interview, you are making the commitment to complete the biggest purchase of your life. The decision to borrow the money to purchase a home is not one you should take lightly. The choices you make during the mortgage process will affect the lives of you and your family for years to come. When you walk into an application meeting, you are asking to be lead by the loan officer into a mortgage program. The ability to ask insightful questions during the process will assist you in gaining a sense of comfort with the process and place the burden of proving their competence on the loan officer. All of the items suggested show an interest and knowledge of the industry on your part. The series of questions also serves to remove some of the pressure from your shoulders by turning the process around somewhat.

The truth is there are many lenders out there and you want to be certain you employ the loan officer who is the correct one for you. You are interviewing the lender and the particular loan officer with whom you are planning to work.

Being offered a loan with a low down payment and low interest rate is only a benefit to you if you have a loan officer and lending office that will follow through and actually provide the promised loan on the day of closing. Many times, the loan terms you finalize at the closing table bear little resemblance to the offer initially quoted to you by the lender when you made your first inquiry. It is imperative that you establish a close working relationship with a competent loan officer whose office has the ability and a proven history of providing the loan funding that they initially promise to you.

You can use the sample questions or customize the questions to meet your particular situation. Just make sure that you ask questions. You are the important one in the home buying and borrowing situation and you must be well informed and comfortable.

- What is the history of <u>Institution Name</u>?

  Many Lending Institutions have undergone mergers and changes in over the past few years. You should pay close attention to the history of the lender as it can tell you of some changes that may occur in the company's policies and procedures during your loan process. If a merger is planned, you will want to ensure that the new company's structure will suit your needs as much as the current company with whom you are speaking.

- How many programs do you have available?

  A lender is only as effective as the programs that he or she has available.

  Whether you are working with a bank or a brokerage, it is important to establish that the available repertoire of programs will meet all your lending needs.

Finding exactly the correct loan program can save you hundreds of dollars a year.

A loan officer who quickly puts you in a standard FHA mortgage with minimal money down and a monthly PMI payment may not be providing you the best possible service.

Another loan officer who spends a day or two researching the programs for your specific situation and then offers you a piggyback 1st mortgage of 80% and second mortgage of 20% with no PMI may be offering a better service for you.

This second scenario may take longer for the loan officer to initially structure. This extra time investment will save you your down payment funds for your future financial needs and actually lower your monthly payment – even if the interest rate on both loans is the same.

PMI or Private Mortgage Insurance is explained later in the manual. Paying PMI has no effect on the principal balance of your mortgage and is therefore a "lost fund" of money you pay monthly until you have achieved a greater equity or ownership interest in your home.

- What are your standard fees and costs?

  This question does not refer only to the commission the loan officer may charge you on a mortgage but also to the amount of money that the branch regularly charges on every loan program that they process.

  There may be a standard underwriting review fee or a processing fee. You will want to review the good faith estimate section of this manual. This chapter allows you to familiarize yourself with fees and determine whom you are paying with every entry on the estimate.

  To pay one point on a $100,000 loan is $1,000! Paying more then one point can dramatically increase the money that you need for closing. On the other hand, paying points could potentially lower your interest rate and save you money over the life of the loan. Most people have heard of paying points on a loan; however, there will be other costs entered into your good faith estimate beyond just the points.

If you pay a $400 underwriting fee a $300 processing fee and a $300 document preparation fee, you are paying the same $1,000 as you would for a point, but these fees do not alter the interest rate you receive. You need to know what fees you are paying and exactly what effect these fees have on your final loan.

In addition to all of that, points are often wrapped into the interest rate. We all know that we should seek out the best interest rate, but few of us understand why the interest rate can vary so greatly from one office to the next. The different rate offerings often occur because the lender, broker, or loan officer is being paid on what is known as the back-end. The chapter regarding interest rates will assist you in gaining the background knowledge you will need to understand the answer you will receive from this question.

Each of these questions gives you examples of items you may want to discuss with a specific loan officer. While reading this manual, be sure to note any other questions as they occur to you. You may not ask all of the questions of your potential loan officer but you will see, as we move through this training program, that there is a lot more involved in a loan program than the standard "What is the rate?" question most people ask.

Pre-qualification
What do they need to know?

From the moment you first speak with a prospective loan provider, they should be gathering information and planning how to close your loan. Many borrowers make those first important calls to loan officers without preparing the information that will be needed to adequately assess and structure the loan possibilities for which you may qualify. A loan officer can only customize a loan for your situation if they understand your situation.

On the next page, you will find a "Pre-approval Questionnaire". The loan officer should use a similar data-gathering device. Completing the questionnaire will help you to answer the questions that the loan officer should ask during your initial telephone call or during the application meeting.

There is a great deal of information conveyed during the pre-qualification call or meeting. This information aids in the loan placement process. A loan officer can only be as competent as you allow them to be. If you do not provide the loan officer with all of the information they will need to assist you in the process, errors in loan structuring and placement are likely to occur.

It is the job of the loan officer to perform their functions in a competent and professional manner. It is your responsibility to provide the loan officer with the information and tools that they need to do so.

It is suggested that you obtain a copy of your credit report and review it with the prospective loan officer prior to authorizing them to pull an additional credit report. Later in chapter "understanding credit reports", we will explain why credit scores are impacted by inquiries. For now, it is important to remember that each time a prospective lender pulls your credit report the inquiry may have an impact on your credit scores.

Many loan product approvals are based upon credit score levels so any action that negatively influences your score should be avoided. A loan officer should be able to begin planning potential loan product options based upon the information you have available in your credit report without needing to pull a separate one for their files. After you have determined the lender that is right for you is the time to allow them access to your social security number for pulling a credit report.

Pre-Qualification Questionnaire

Borrower Name: _____ Co-Borrower Name: _____

Home Phone: _____ Other Phone: _____ Best time(s) to call: _____

DOB: _____ SSN: _____ DOB: _____ SSN: _____

May I run a credit report?___ Yes ___ No   May I run a credit report? ___ Yes ___ No

Employer: _____   Employer: _____

Address: _____   Address: _____

Phone: _____ No yrs. ___ Position: _____ Phone: _____ No yrs. ___ Position: _____

Current Address: _____

Landlord/Mortgage Holder: _____ Phone: _____

Rent ____ Own ___ Number of Years at Present Address _____

Have you chosen a home to purchase? ___ Yes ___ No Cost $_____

Gross Income		Debt	
Borrowers Mthly	$_____	Mortgage/Rental Payment	$_____
Prev Year	$_____	Auto Payment	$_____
Co-Borrowers Mthly	$_____	Auto Payment #2	$_____
Prev Year	$_____	Installment Debt_____	$_____
Other Income _____	$_____	Installment Debt _____	$_____
Other Income _____	$_____	Other _____	$_____
Total Income	$_____	Total Debt	$_____

Explanation of Investment or Credit Situation/Notes:

Pre-qualification Questionnaire Key

Borrower Name Co-Borrower Name	You will need to include your full name including middle initial and any additional information Jr., Sr., II. Do not use nicknames; however, you should note any aliases that you have commonly used. Names, especially among family, can be very similar. The more identifying information you can provide the more pure your credit report will be. In some instances, you will not have a co-borrower. When you do, it is as important to provide correct identifying information for this person as it is for yourself.
Date of Birth/Social Security Number	This information is important for your loan application and vital when you are having a credit report pulled. Always ask that the credit reports be run separately. Even if you are married, you will want to have separate reports. There are times you will want to drop one person's credit and application information in an effort to improve the loan that you receive.
May I run a credit report?	It is imperative that you answer this question. No one is allowed to run a credit report on any individual without his or her prior consent. You must sign a credit consent form before the report is completed. Remember that each time your credit report is pulled it could potentially affect your credit score. Only provide authorization to have your report pulled once you have completed shopping for a lender and decided whom you prefer to use.
Employer	This information aids the loan officer in determining some of the issues that may arise during the course of the loan. You will need to provide a 2-year employment history and account for any time that you were not employed. You should also note any time you spent obtaining education for your current job. In some instances of unusual history, the loan officer may want to use bank statements to prove income.

Number of years at present employment	The loan officer is looking for a minimum of two years employment history. If you have not been in your current employment two years, you will need to trace back under comments until you have submitted a complete two-year history. This is an excellent place for the loan officer to refer to when your loan application requires an exception. If something in your profile is not quite what the loan underwriter needs to approve your application, the loan officer may be able to use compensating factors to help gain the approval that you need. A common compensating factor is 'at current employment more than 5 years.'
Current Address	This is identifying information you will want to provide to clarify your identity on the credit report.
Landlord/Mortgage Holder	It is important to determine from the start if you pay an entity or an individual. Your payment history to an entity can be verified via a form called a VOR/VOM, which the loan officer will acquire, but if you make payments to an individual, the underwriter may require 12 months cancelled checks for verification of payment history.
Rent/Own	This question begins to draw a picture of the possible source of funds as well as the type of loan you may require.
Number of years?	You will need a two-year residence history for each borrower on the application. If you have been at your current residence less than two years, you will need to add in comments any additional residence history until you have completed two years. This is an excellent place for the loan officer to refer to when your application requires an exception. A common compensating factor is 'at current residence more than 5 years.'
Have you chosen a property to purchase?	This allows the lender to rank your loan status by urgency. If you have chosen your property, the loan will take precedence over those applications that are just beginning the buying process.

Value	This allows the lender get an idea of your expectations based on the price range you are considering. This figure will be used to determine if the property you are considering fits into your DTI (debt to income ratio). Often borrowers are very high or very low in their estimate of what they can spend.
Type of Loan: 1st Mortgage, 2nd Mortgage, Rate or Term Refinance, Cash-out Refinance	Knowing the types of loans you believe you desire allows the loan officer to begin planning the loan structure and matrix placement from the moment of query. You will find product approvals vary greatly depending on the type of loan you choose.
Income Information	In order to pre-qualify a package the loan officer must have complete income information. Many loans are denied based on excessive DTI Ratios. All income should be entered even if you do not wish to use all of this income as qualifying income. At times, some income cannot be used as qualifying income. Your loan officer will assist you in making a determination as to the income that will be applicable for your situation.
Debt Information	Debt load will be visible on the Credit Report but it is important to verify this information. There may be debt that is not yet showing on the report but may crop up before closing the loan. Child support payments do affect the debt load. The debt load that you currently carry compared to your income will affect how much money you can borrow. It is important that you tell the loan officer about any payments you make on a regular basis.
Explanation of current situation?	This is the opportunity for notes. You always want to explain any information that is present on your credit report. Your credit history is an essential factor in loan approval. If you are aware of a negative item on your credit report, telling your loan officer early in the process can help the loan officer in placing your loan.

3

Understanding the Credit Report & DTI

It is important that you understand the credit report and the potential impact the information contained on the report may have on the outcome of the transaction.

Every action a consumer takes affects their credit report. These actions can have a negative or a positive effect.

Credit reports are an overview of your entire history of spending and payment habits. Almost everything that you do financially is reported, collected, and stored in the credit profile. The primary concern of a lender is any action that had a negative or derogatory impact on your credit history.

Debt: The term describing any situation in which funds are borrowed.

Debt Load: The amount of debt that you are carrying (owe).

                      Debt load may include many items. The most common being:

- Credit card debt
- Department store debt
- Charge accounts

- Auto loans
- Student loans
- Mortgages

The ability to borrow more money or to have additional credit extended is effected by how much debt you currently carry.

A lender will be concerned with debt-to-income ratio.

Debt-to-Income Ratio's: The amount of open debt weighed against your monthly income.

The higher the DTI the greater the potential risk of a default on the loan.

The credit report will provide a relatively accurate view of current debt load. You should review the debts listed on your credit report. If any debt showing on the report does not belong to you or if you have debt that does not show on the report, you will want to bring it to the attention of your loan officer.

Late payments: Any payments that have been paid more than 30 days past the due date are considered late payments.

Late payments can be a severe blemish on your credit report.

A late payment will appear on the credit report for two years, though credit bureaus may keep them in the credit file for up to seven years.

Bankruptcy: Bankruptcy can remain on the credit report for as long as 10 years.

To borrow in the prime market you may have to wait up to four years from the date of your bankruptcy discharge to attempt to qualify for most loans. You must also re-establish a credit history during that time. This re-establishment of credit will aid in showing that you are no longer a credit risk.

The sub-prime market is more lenient as to time that must elapse before obtaining mortgage finance after a bankruptcy. The sub-prime market is also more lenient concerning the amount of credit you must establish before seeking mortgage financing. The sub-prime market gains their security through higher interest rates and fees.

Collection accounts: Accounts that a borrower has failed to pay as agreed are usually turned over to a collection department or agency in the attempt to collect the payments owed. The initial creditor and the collection agencies report these accounts to the bureaus.

If you have collection accounts in your credit-profile, you will likely need to resolve them before you can get a mortgage loan. If you have already paid these debts in full, obtain a letter stating that the debt has been completely satisfied and no further action on your part or by the creditor is necessary.

Medical collections: Accounts to medical service providers that have not been paid can also become collection accounts.

Medical Collection Accounts are often treated differently than other collection accounts.

Your loan officer will review any collection accounts on your credit report and explain to you how they need to be handled in order for you to qualify for a loan.

Credit inquiries: Accesses to the credit profile are called credit inquiries.

These inquiries are visible on the credit report.

A series of inquiries could also indicate that new credit obligations are present but not visible on the report. You will need to explain any recent credit inquiries to your loan officer.

Credit Bureau Scores: Scores generated based solely on credit bureau data are called Fair Isaac Credit Scores or FICO for short.

Credit Bureau Scores are one of the many elements that are reshaping today's mortgage industry. Credit Bureau scoring is a scientific way of assessing how likely a borrower is to pay back a loan.

Credit Scores are used extensively in such industries as mortgage lending, auto lending, and bankcards.

The loan program and interest rate you are offered will depend, in part, on your credit score.

Your loan officer will review your credit scores and should explain the reason for your score to you when you meet for an interview.

How is the CBS calculated?

A Credit Bureau Score is based on the data available in your credit report.

The score measures the relative degree of risk you represent to the lender or investor.

A credit bureau score is not a measure of your income, assets, or bank account. These factors are taken into consideration by lenders and investors independent of credit scores.

Score Range:

FICO scores range from approximately 450 to 850 points.

Score Data:

The types of credit information used in the credit bureau scorecards include some of the same items that the lender will use to make a credit decision. These can include:

- Payment history
- Public records and collection items
- Severity, recentness, and frequency of delinquencies noted in the trade line section
- Outstanding Debt
- Number of balances recently reported
- Average balance across all trade lines

- Relationship between total balances and total credit limits on revolving trade lines
- Credit History
- Age of oldest trade line
- Inquiries and new account openings
- Number of inquiries in the last year
- Number of new accounts opened in the last year
- Amount of time since most recent inquiry
- Types of credit in use
- Number of trade lines for each type:

> Bankcard
>
> Travel and Entertainment cards
>
> Department store cards
>
> Personal finance company references
>
> Installment loans
>
> Other credit

Fair Isaac observes tens of thousands of credit report histories of mortgage borrowers to determine which credit report items or combination of items are the most predictive of future risk. This data indicates the amount of weight each item should contribute to a credit decision. Your loan officer will have guidelines regarding credit scores for each loan program that they have to offer.

FAIR, ISAAC CREDIT BUREAU SCORES DO NOT USE RACE, COLOR, RELIGION, NATIONAL ORIGIN, SEX, MARITAL STATUS, OR AGE AS PREDICTIVE CHARACTERISTICS.

OCCUPATION AND LENGTH OF TIME IN PRESENT HOUSING ARE ALSO NOT USED IN THE SCORECARDS.

ANY INFORMATION THAT IS NOT PRESENT IN THE CREDIT FILE IS NOT USED IN CREATING A CREDIT BUREAU SCORECARD.

Understanding a score's impact

A Fair, Isaac Credit Bureau Score is a means of rank-ordering potential borrowers based on the likelihood that they will pay their credit obligations as agreed.

A higher score indicates a better credit quality. If all other things are equal, borrowers with a score of 640 are less likely to default on a loan than borrowers with a score of 560.

The Fair, Isaac Credit Bureau Score models at each credit repository is of similar design and the scores are scaled to indicate a similar level of risk across all three repositories. In other words, a score of 660 at one bureau will represent a similar level of risk as a score of 660 at another bureau.

The risk is defined in terms of the number of accounts that remain in good standing compared to those that default.

Credit score ranges for new mortgage borrowers from a national sample

Score Range serious	Number of good loans for each bad loan showing delinquency or foreclosure (# of good to 1 bad)
Below 600	8 to 1

700 – 719	123 to 1
Above 800	1,292 to 1

Figure 3:1 Credit Score Ranges and Results

Credit Bureau Scores will rank-order potential borrowers based on risk or the number of good loans to bad loans denoted by a score. This rank ordering is likely to fluctuate due to changes in the economy, regional differences, changes in product offerings or other reasons.

A lender using credit scores will compare performance of their loans by score over time to determine the relationship of score and performance for their own market environment. The in-house determination may alter the impact your scores have on the final loan approval.

Report Appearance

Credit reports can take multiple visual forms depending on the bureau that issued the report and the type of record that was requested. Regardless of the initial visual variations, all credit reports contain the same basic elements. These include your details and data, a summary of all of the credit inclusions, and a detailed breakdown of your current and historical credit transactions. Each section of the report will contain details that will assist the lender in determining if you will qualify for one of their loan programs.

The upper portion of credit report will typically include identifying related to the individual or company who requested your report.

Report type will usually be included in the header. Report type may be individual or joint.

Information relating to the individual within the credit bureau who pulled the report and the internal case ID # assigned to the report will be defined in the header of the report. This information will be important if your lender must request updates to the report or address a discrepancy in the report with the credit bureau.

MERGED INFILE CREDIT REPORT

Prepared For:	Property Address:	Prepared By:	Date Rec:
Attention:	Loan Type: Purpose of Loan: Report Type:	Computer ID: Case #:	Date Comp: Date Revised:

	APPLICANT		CO-APPLICANT	
Name: SSN: Marital Status: Home Phone: Present Address:	 DOB: Dependents:	Name: SSN: Marital Status: Home Phone: Present Address:	 DOB: Dependents:
Since:	Own / Rent	Since:	Own / Rent
Previous Address:		Previous Address:	
From: To:	Own / Rent	From: To:	Own / Rent

Date data will be included within the report. Date data can include the date the request was received by the credit bureau, the date the credit bureau completed the report, and the date of any revisions created by the credit bureau in relationship to the report.

Date is important because the lender typically stipulates that the report must be current, or within a certain date range, in order to be used for closing.

If the report is out of date, the lender will request a new report in order to ensure that no changes have occurred in your credit profile during the processing stage of the loan. You should caution that you do not to make any large purchases or take any action that may alter the contents of the report until after the loan has closed.

Figure 3:2 Example - Credit Report Extract / Explanation

Borrower Information

The credit report will contain details relating to the individual or individuals to whom the credit report applies.

This portion includes specifics such as your full name, social security number, and date of birth. Information relating to your address and employment may be included in this segment of the report.

Variations in the address and employment information from your current information are common within the report. You should note any discrepancy report and inform your loan officer that it may not be correct. This helps the loan officer ensure that the report does not contain entries that relate to another individual with a similar name.

MERGED INFILE CREDIT REPORT

Prepared For:	Property Address:	Prepared By:	Date Rec:
Attention:	Loan Type: Purpose of Loan: Report Type:	Computer ID: Lender Case #:	Date Comp: Date Revised:

APPLICANT	CO-APPLICANT
Name: SSN: DOB: Marital Status: Dependents:: Home Phone: Present Address: Since: Own / Rent Previous Address: From: To: Own / Rent	Name: SSN: DOB: Marital Status: Dependents: Home Phone: Present Address: Since: Own / Rent Previous Address: From: To: Own / Rent

Borrower and Co-Borrower identifying information is entered in this section.

You should verify that all details entered on the credit report are correct.

Figure 3:3 Sample Credit Report Explanation

Credit Summary

The credit report will contain a segment that summarizes the details contained within the actual report. You should review this area to ensure that all of the information is correct and current. If you note an issue, you should bring it to the attention of your loan officer.

CREDIT SUMMARY

	PAYMENTS	BALANCES	LIMITS	TRADES	30+	60+	90+
REVOLVING	0	2061	2200	4	4	4	17
INSTALLMENT 1307	1307	79365	90610	25	34	8	27
REAL ESTATE	378	35384	36600	1	2	0	0
OPEN/OTHER	991	1041	1041	5	0	0	0
TOTAL	2676	117851	129451	38	40	12	44

# INQUIRIES	50	# PUBLIC RECORDS	0	# BANKRUPTCIES	0
WORST TRADE	9	OLDEST DATE	07/01/89	# SATISFACTORIES	17

The summary will contain details identifying the types of credit that you have available.

Credit payment totals and current balances will appear within the credit summary portion of the report.

You will confirm the payment information when you review the report inclusions.

A summary data analysis of the details of the report will be included. This analysis will assist you in completing the scoring key. Much of the data you will use during credit scoring will be summarized with in this section. Before you export the data into the credit-scoring key, debt-to-income ratio form, or application, you must review the report with the buyer to ensure that all of the inclusions of the summary are correct and relate to active accounts.

Figure 3:4 Sample Credit Report Explanation

CREDIT SUMMARY

	PAYMENTS	BALANCE	LIMITS	TRADE	30+	60+	90+
REVOLVING	0	2061	2200	4	4	4	17
INSTALLMENT 1307	1307	79365	90610	25	34	8	27
REAL ESTATE	378	35384	36600	1	2	0	0
OPEN/OTHER	991	1041	1041	5	0	0	0
TOTAL	2676	117851	129451	38	40	12	44

# INQUIRIES	50	# PUBLIC RECORDS	0	# BANKRUPTCIES	0
WORST TRADE	9	OLDEST DATE 07/01/89		# SATISFACTORIES	17

The number of inquiries into your credit profile will be totaled and entered into the summary.

A detailed breakdown of the companies that made credit inquiries will be included at the end of the report.

You may be required to provide an explanation for any excessive inquiries.

Credit inquiries may indicate that you have additional debt that is not yet showing on the credit report or may be related to the search for mortgage financing.

If you are not aware of the reason for the recent inquiries, this may be an indication of fraud and you should review all of the entries on your report in case you are a victim of identity theft.

Specifics regarding public records, bankruptcy, and the worst trade payment history will be included within the credit summary.

You should review these entries to ensure that the details of the report contain the correct information.

Each funding source will have specific requirements related to public records, bankruptcy actions, and poor credit history.

Figure 3:5 Example - Credit Report Extract

CREDIT SUMMARY

	PAYMENTS	BALANCE	LIMITS	TRADES	30+	60+	90+
REVOLVING	0	2061	2200	4	4	4	17
INSTALLMENT	1307	79365	90610	25	34	8	27
REAL ESTATE	378	35384	36600	1	2	0	0
OPEN/OTHER	991	1041	1041	5	0	0	0
TOTAL 2676	117851	129451		38	40	12	44

# INQUIRIES 50	# PUBLIC RECORDS 0	# BANKRUPTCIES 0
WORST TRADE 9	OLDEST DATE 07/01/89	# SATISFACTORIES 17

The oldest date field indicates the date that you fist obtained credit.

This inclusion allows your loan officer to ensure that an adequate credit history is available to you. Many loan guidelines will require you have at least a two-year credit history with at least three open active trade lines. If you do not have a sufficient credit history or quantity of accounts, you and your loan officer may need to take alternative actions to create a credit profile that meets the minimum requirements of the funding guidelines.

An alternative credit profile could include any payments that you make on a regular basis but that are not reported to the credit agency. Trash or other utility services, cell phone payments, rent to own payments, or similar items could all be included when building an alternative credit history.

Figure 3:6 Example - Credit Report Extract

Score Factors

The name of the repository issuing the credit score included with the report will be included.

The lending guidelines will designate which of the 3 credit repository scores is applicable for you.

This designation is a result of regional variations regarding reported matters making one repository more complete than another does.

The code of the applicable agency will be entered to confirm the source of the score.

EFX = Equifax

8   BEACON SCORE   EFX01
519
SERIOUS DELINQUENCY AND DEROGATORY PUBLIC RECORD OR COLLECTION FILED
AMOUNT OWED ON DELINQUENT ACCOUNTS
PROPORTION OF BALANCES TO CREDIT LIMITS TOO HIGH ON REVOLVING ACCOUNTS
LENGTH OF TIME ACCOUNTS HAVE BEEN ESTABLISHED

8   EMPIRICA SCORE   TRU01
493
SERIOUS DELINQUENCY, AND PUBLIC RECORD OR COLLECTION FILED
LEVEL OF DELINQUENCY ON ACCOUNTS
TIME SINCE DELINQUENCY IS TOO RECENT OR UNKNOWN
PROPORTION OF REVOLVING BALANCES TO REVOLVING CREDIT LIMITS IS TOO HIGH

8   FAIR ISAAC SCORE   XPN01
529
SERIOUS DELINQUENCY AND PUBLIC RECORD OR COLLECTION FILED
PROPORTION OF BALANCES TOO HIGH ON REVOLVING ACCOUNTS
NUMBER OF ACCOUNTS DELINQUENT
LENGTH OF TIME SINCE LEGAL ITEM FILED OR COLLECTION ITEM REPORTED

The factors that affect the score will be included on the report. This information is often referred to as score factor code.

Figure 37 Example - Credit Report Extract

Score Factors – Reason Codes

To understand why your credit report scored the way it did, you must review the reason codes given within each score. These reason codes provide the top reasons why you did not score higher. These scores are only the top reasons and other factors probably contribute to the overall score. You should review both the score and the reasons the score ranks where it does.

To find the score reason codes you should locate a number or a letter followed by a brief description.

For example, a score of 540 may have the following factors:

> 02 – Delinquency on accounts
>
> 01 – Amount owed on accounts is too high
>
> 09 – Too many accounts opened in the last 12 months
>
> 19 – Too few accounts currently paid as agreed

Score factors are less meaningful for higher scoring credit records as they merely point to the reasons why a very good credit report was not perfect.

Examples of adverse factors that may appear on the report as a consideration in the score calculation are:

- Current outstanding balances on accounts
- Delinquency report on accounts
- Accounts not paid as agreed
- Too few open accounts
- Too many open accounts
- Too many bank accounts with outstanding balances
- Too many finance company accounts
- Payment history too new to rate

- Number of inquiries within the last 12 months
- Number of accounts opened within the last 12 months
- Balance too high
- Length of credit history
- No recent account information
- Too few accounts rate as current
- Amount past due on accounts
- No adverse factors
- Recent derogatory public record or collection

This is not an all-inclusive listing. The items listed are examples of issues you may find in the score coding section of a report. You should review your report carefully to determine the factors specific to that credit profile.

Fraud Alert

The fraud alert field is becoming increasingly filled field within today's environment. Any data that indicates possible fraud activity will be included with in this section. The information will often become a warning entry because of some action that you have taken but any entry other than "*available and clear*" should be reviewed and discussed with the loan officer.

Basic information noted by the credit bureau as potential fraud will be flagged.

If the entry is not related to an action that you have taken, you may be a victim of identity theft and all entries in the body of the report should be scrutinized to ensure that all of the accounts do belong to you

An example of a fraud alert entry would be the number of inquiries in the last 60 days.

Excessive inquiries may be a result of your mortgage shopping process. In this case, there is little cause for concern as the alert is related to an action that you have taken. Excessive inquiries could indicate access to the credit profile by another party who is seeking to open fraudulent accounts in your name.

FRAUD ALERT

1   TRANS ALERT   TRU01
               # INQUIRIES IN LAST 60 DAYS: 04
               RECORDED INQUIRIES ALERT

1   HAWK ALERT   TRU 01
               HAWK AVAILABLE AND CLEAR

Details regarding any activity that may indicate fraud will be included.

AVAILABLE AND CLEAR   =   No information found

inquiries in the last 60 days   =   potential credit gathering spree or identity theft

Figure 3:8 Sample Credit Report Explanation

CREDIT HISTORY DETAILS

The main body of the report will contain details of each account contained within the borrower's credit history. You will wish to scrutinize each entry within this section to determine the status of the borrower's credit, gain an understanding of the borrower payment and spending habits, and complete the credit history-scoring key.

The credit history-scoring key will be explained later and is included within the appendix section of your workbook. This key will assist you in extracting the necessary details from the credit profile.

CREDIT HISTORY

E C O A	CREDITOR ACCOUNT NO	DATE RPTED	DATE LAST ACT	DATE OPND	LIMIT / HIGHEST CREDIT	PRESENT STATUS		TERMS	PAY AMT	TYPE AND ACCT STATUS	HISTORICAL STATUS			
						BALANCE OWING	AMOUNT PAST DUE				NO MOS HIIST REV	3 0	60	9 0
8	AFM-BLOOM #APRINTLO COLLECTION	02/99	04/94		425	425				OPN05				

Figure 3:9 Sample Credit Report Explanation

The name of the creditor and the account number will be included within the report.

Account numbers are often shortened on the credit report and the full account number may not appear. You can obtain the full account number from your statements if it is a necessary element of the loan process.

For example, a refinance transaction may require certain bills to be paid in full as part of the transaction. You will need to provide the full account number for each account so that your loan officer can confirm the pay off amount and to ensure that all payments are allocated correctly at the closing.

CREDIT HISTORY

E C O A	CREDITOR ACCOUNT NO	DATE RPTD	DATE LAST ACT	DATE OPND	LIMIT / HIGHEST CREDIT	PRESENT STATUS		PAY AMT	TYPE AND ACCT STATUS	HISTORICAL STATUS			
						BAL OWING	AMT PAST DUE			NO MOS HIIST REV	3 0	6 0	9 0
8	AFM-BLOOM #APRINTLO COLLECTION	02/9 9	04/94		425	425			OPN05				

The date reported is the last reporting date for a particular account.

Not all creditors report on a monthly basis.

You may be required to provide the loan officer with data pertaining to a specific account to comply with underwriting guidelines.

This up date status helps to ensure that no new derogatory data exists during the last months of the account,

The date last active information provides details relating to the last date that the account was in use.

Some accounts will be old, closed accounts and will not affect the current transaction.

You should review the last active date to ensure that all closed accounts show as closed on your report. Open accounts will affect your debt ratio.

The opening date of the account allows you to review the historical status with more accuracy.

Figure 2:11 Example - Credit Report Extract / Explanation

The present status details the current balances and any amounts currently due for each account.

You should scan this column to note any information that is not correct.

Past due accounts may lead to a credit denial or change in the terms of credit offered to you for your new home loan.

The terms field shows the original and the current agreement relating to the payments and terms of each account.

A revolving account or credit card will typically not provide you with the end date for the payments since these accounts will continue until one party cancels the relationship.

Installment notes will show the payment terms agreed upon between you and the lender for each account.

Payment amount will show the minimum payment that is due for each account.

These payment amount will be used to calculate your DTI ratio.

If the account has no payment entered, it may be an inactive account or it may be a revolving account that does not have a balance.

Even if an account does not have a balance, if credit is available to you, the lender will factor a minimum payment into the debt ratio for that account.

CREDIT HISTORY

ECOA	CREDITOR ACCOUNT NO	DATE RPTD	DATE LAST ACT	DATE OPND	LIMIT / HIGHEST CREDIT	PRESENT STATUS		PAY AMT	TYPE AND ACCT STATUS	HISTORICAL STATUS			
						BAL OWING	AMT PAST DUE			NO MOS HIIST REV	3 0	6 0	9 0
8	AFM-BLOOM #APRINTLO COLLECTION	02/9 9	04/94		425	425			OPN05				

Figure 3:12 Sample Credit Report Explanation

Type and account status will provide information defining the type of account and its present status.

- Revolving   REV
- Installment Ins
- Mortgage   Mtg
- Consumer   Cons

This field could also contain derogatory accounts such as collections, charge offs or judgments.

- The number of month's history shows the numbers of months reported on the history of the account.

  Your loan program guidelines will dictate the number of months that must be reviewed for each account.

- When your loan officer reviews the account, they will be seeking the status of the account.

  In other words, they will review the account to determine whether the payments were made on time or if any late payment exists within the history.

- They will also look for the date of each payment.

  The loan program you select may have account history requirements. Some programs require that your credit report shows at least 3 open active accounts or that you have at least a 2-year credit history before you can obtain a mortgage loan.

- The historical status and late payments section provides the loan officer with numerical entries that indicate any late payments that will be found within the report.

Each account history will contain numbers indicating the status of a particular month's payment.

1 = on time

2 = 30 days late

3 = 60 days late

X = the same status as the previous month

This section of the history summary will provide the loan officer with the number of times you have been on time, 30 days, 60 days, or 90 days late during the reported credit history.

An account shows a 1 indicates that the account was paid on time within the history.

➢ When the loan officer notes an account that contains derogatory information or a credit blemish, they will first confirm that the account is active, that the derogatory entry is recent and that the entry applies to the process.

➢ They will determine the last date that the account was reported and begin counting backwards from the last entry.

They will review the account details by moving from left to right.

Example: The reporting of this account begins in July.

The first entry is July. Moving backwards from Left to Right the next entries are

June	=	On Time
May	=	30 Days Late
April	=	On Time

and then backwards through time all of the payments were made on time.

Example: The next account was reported in June so the backwards counting will begin with the month of June.

The loan officer would need to obtain an update for this account that illustrates the payment in July to bring this account current with the other entries on the report.

The loan officer will review each entry on your credit report and create a scoring key that helps them determine if your credit history meets the minimum credit requirements for the loan programs that they have available. Your credit history will influence the type of loan you can obtain, the interest rate you will pay on the loan, the down payment you will need for the purchase and other factors.

Increasing the Score

Over time, you can improve the information in your credit report by paying credit obligations as agreed and using credit wisely. As derogatory data in the credit report gets older, it affects the score less. A missed payment from four years ago will not count as much as a missed payment from six months ago. As you use your credit in a more controlled manner, keeping debt load well below your maximum credit limits, your score is also likely to increase.

A credit score, like a credit report, is a snapshot of your changing credit record. If you make a request for a second repository report to get an updated score, the score is likely to change for many reasons. It is not possible to control how that score will change.

The credit items on the report are updated often, so new items are likely to have been added since the previous report. Repeatedly requesting the credit report may substantially increase the number of inquiries on the repository report, which may affect the score adversely.

Removing Erroneous Information

If you believe there is erroneous information on your credit report, you should contact the credit-reporting agency that developed the report. The Fair Credit Reporting Act (FCRA) allows the credit-reporting agency a "reasonable period of time", generally not to exceed 30 days, to investigate disputed items.

A significant number of credit grantors use an automated system for investigating the disputes and respond to the dispute within a few days. Most credit reporting agencies make a special effort to resolve disputed information affecting a mortgage decision.

Because the score uses all the credit-related data on the credit bureau report and takes into account all contributing factors, removing or changing one specific, derogatory item will not guarantee an increase in your score. In some cases, a change in the credit bureau report will have little or no effect on the score. Because there are many scorecards using a complex mathematical formula at each of the repositories, it is not possible to estimate how much the score will change if specific derogatory information is removed for a single repository report.

The number of inquiries may or may not be a factor in the score. When inquiries are a factor, they are typically not a strong one.

The law requires a record of all inquiries into the file be kept on file. This means an inquiry cannot be removed from the credit report. Consumer disclosure inquiries are not used in determining score.

MERGED INFILE CREDIT REPORT

Prepared For:	Property Address:	Prepared By:	Date Rec:
Attention:	Loan Type:	Computer ID:	Date Comp:
	Purpose of Loan:		
	Report Type:	Lender Case #:	Date Revised:

APPLICANT	CO-APPLICANT
Name: SSN: DOB: Marital Status: Dependents: Home Phone: Present Address: Since: Own / Rent Previous Address: From: To: Own / Rent	Name: SSN: DOB: Marital Status: Dependents: Home Phone: Present Address: Since: Own / Rent Previous Address: From: To: Own / Rent

CREDIT SUMMARY

	PAYMENTS	BALANCES	LIMITS	TRADES	30+	60+	90+
REVOLVING	0	2061	2200	4	4	4	17
INSTALLMENT	1307	1307	79365	25	34	8	27
REAL ESTATE	378	35384	36600	1	2	0	0
OPEN/OTHER	991	1041	1041	5	0	0	0
TOTAL	2676	117851	129451	38	40	12	44

# INQUIRIES 50	# PUBLIC RECORDS 0	# BANKRUPTCIES 0
WORST TRADE 9	OLDEST DATE 07/01/89	# SATISFACTORIES 17

2	JUDGEMENT SRCE – 1011 LACT – 09/96	RPTD – 09/96 AMT – 13245 PLTF –	VRFD - ASSET -	OPND – LIAB -	CASE – 104 BAL - XPN01
1	JUDGEMENT SRCE – 1016	RPTD – 11/94 AMT – 1900	VRFD - ASSET -	OPND – LIAB -	CASE – 9401 BAL -

LACT – 01/95   PLTF -   XPN01

8   BEACON SCORE   EFX01
        519
        SERIOUS DELINQUENCY AND DEROGATORY PUBLIC RECORD OR COLLECTION
FILED
        AMOUNT OWED ON DELINQUENT ACCOUNTS
        PROPORTION OF BALANCES TO CREDIT LIMITS TOO HIGH ON REVOLVING
ACCOUNTS
        LENGTH OF TIME ACCOUNTS HAVE BEEN ESTABLISHED

8   EMPIRICA SCORE   TRU01
        493
        SERIOUS DELINQUENCY, AND PUBLIC RECORD OR COLLECTION FILED
        LEVEL OF DELINQUENCY ON ACCOUNTS
        TIME SINCE DELINQUENCY IS TOO RECENT OR UNKNOWN
        PROPORTION OF REVOLVING BALANCES TO REVOLVING CREDIT LIMITS IS TOO
HIGH

8   FAIR ISAAC SCORE   XPN01
        529
        SERIOUS DELINQUENCY AND PUBLIC RECORD OR COLLECTION FILED
        PROPORTION OF BALANCES TOO HIGH ON REVOLVING ACCOUNTS
        NUMBER OF ACCOUNTS DELINQUENT
        LENGTH OF TIME SINCE LEGAL ITEM FILED OR COLLECTION ITEM REPORTED

CREDIT HISTORY

E C O A	CREDITOR ACCOUNT NO	DATE RPTED	DATE LAST ACT	DATE OPND	LIMIT / HIGHEST CREDIT	PRESENT STATUS		TERMS	PAY AMT	TYPE AND ACCT STATUS	HISTORICAL STATUS			
						BALANCE OWING	AMOUNT PAST DUE				NO MOS HIIST REV	30	60	90
8	AFM-BLOOM #APRINTLO COLLECTIO	02/99	04/94		425	425				OPN05	132111111 TRU01			
8	BENEFICL-HFC #7101702	07/00	04/00	03/97	0	0	0	39M 125		INS 01	37	0	0	0
										XX1111111X1111111111X XXX111111111111111111 TRU01			
8	CAPTIAL 1 BK 05291071382	04/00	01/00	06/96	592	0	0			REV01	41	0	0	0
										111111111111111111111 111111111111111111111 TRU01			
8	CCB 42270972 CREDIT CARD	07/00	02/00	07/98	950	0				REV01	24	0	0	0
										EFX01			
1	CITIBANK 54241800	06/00	06/00	12/99	3500	3516	0	72	72	REV01	8	0	0	0

ECOA	CREDITOR ACCOUNT NO	DATE RPTED	DATE LAST ACT	DATE OPND	LIMIT / HIGHEST CREDIT	PRESENT STATUS		TERMS	PAY AMT	TYPE AND ACCT STATUS	HISTORICAL STATUS			
						BALANCE OWING	AMOUNT PAST DUE				NO MOS HIST REV	30	60	90
											11111111 TRU01			
8	CORNER STONE S0000070010	09/00	06/96	09/94	4374	0	0	18M 223		INS00	1	0	0	0
											TRU01			
8	DIRECT MERCH BK 54580000114	07/00	07/00	11/95	2600	2496		83	83	REV01	25	0	0	0
											111111111111111111111 111111111111111111111 XPN01			

ECOA	CREDITOR ACCOUNT NO	DATE RPTED	DATE LAST ACT	DATE OPND	LIMIT / HIGHEST CREDIT	PRESENT STATUS		TERMS	PAY AMT	TYPE AND ACCT STATUS	HISTORICAL STATUS			
						BALANCE OWING	AMOUNT PAST DUE				NO MOS HIST REV	30	60	90
8	AFM-BLOOM #APRINTLO COLLEC CLOSED – CONS	02/99	04/94		425	425				OPN05				
											132111111 TRU01			
8	BENEFICL-HFC #7101702 CLOSED	07/00	04/00	03/97	0	0	0	39M 125		INS 01	37	0	0	0
											XX1111111X1111111111X XXX1111111111111111111 TRU01			
8	CAPTIAL 1 BK 05291071382 CLOSED – CONS	04/00	01/00	06/96	592	0	0			REV01	41	0	0	0
											111111111111111111111 111111111111111111111 TRU01			
8	CCB 42270972 CREDIT CARD CREDIT CARD	07/00	02/00	07/98	950	0				REV01	24	0	0	0
											EFX01			
1	CITIBANK 54241800 CREDIT CARD	06/00	06/00	12/99	3500	3516	0	72	72	REV01	8	0	0	0
											11111111 TRU01			
8	CORNER STONE S0000070010 CLOSED AUTO	09/00	06/96	09/94	4374	0	0	18M 223		INS00	1	0	0	0
											TRU01			
8	DIRECT MERCH BK 54580000114 CREDIT CARD	07/00	07/00	11/95	2600	2496		83	83	REV01	25	0	0	0
											111111111111111111111 111111111111111111111 XPN01			
1	FCNB/NEWP 4220507 CHARGE ACCOUNT	07/00	06/00	09/99	900	888		30	30	REV01	10	0	0	0
											111111111111111111111 111111111111111111111 TRU01			
3	FIRST USA BANK NA 5417623 CREDIT CARD	07/00	07/00	12/99	3000	2602	0	65	65	REV01	8	0	0	0
											11111111 TRU01			
2	FNANB 15230035125 CREDIT CARD	09/00	09/00	12/99	3000	1976		79	79	REV01	9	0	0	0
											111111111111111111111 11111 EPN01			
1	FNANB VISA	06/00	06/00	06/98	700	0				REV01	27	1	0	0

54063555013										X11211111111111111111111 EFX01

FRAUD ALERT

1   TRANS ALERT   TRU01
        # INQUIRIES IN LAST 60 DAYS: 04
        RECORDED INQUIRIES ALTER

1   HAWK ALERT   TRU 01
        HAWK AVAILABLE AND CLEAR

Figure 3:12 Sample Credit Report

DEBT-TO-INCOME RATIO'S

The debt ratio is what will determine "how much" loan you can afford. The debt ratio is determined by comparing the current amount of money you owe with your income to determine how much money is left to spend on a monthly basis.

Following are the two types of debt ratios that are often considered:

Front-End Ratio -   This is your gross income divided by the new PITI mortgage payment.

In the conventional mortgage marketplace, the standard guideline is 29% of your gross monthly income. For non-conforming (sub-prime) loan programs, the back-end debt ratio is more often used. This can be as high as 55% of your gross monthly income depending on the loan product being considered.

Back-End Ratio -   This is your gross income divided by the new PITI mortgage payment and the minimum monthly payments from all of your other liabilities.

The standard guideline is 41% and the non-conforming guideline can be as high as 55%.

You may wish to review the debt-to-income ratio before beginning your mortgage search. The DTI Ratio is a common reason you may not obtain the best loan approval. If you understand your debt-to-income ratio and take steps to minimize your expenditures before completing an application process, you may be able to improve your loan approval quality.

Following are the typical debts used to determine the qualifying ratios:

Front-End Ratios

The current and or future house payment

Back-End Ratios

The minimum required monthly payments on all of the following:

Auto Loans - typically discounted if there is less than 9 months left to pay

Student Loans - typically discounted if there is less than 9 months left

Personal Loans - typically discounted if there is less than 9 months left

Charge Cards - only the minimum required payments are used

Child Support - typically discounted if there is less than 9 months left

Alimony - typically discounted if there is less than 9 months left

Federal Tax Lien - repayments may be discounted if there is less than 9 months on the repayment schedule

The following are examples of monthly liabilities that are not used to calculate debt ratios:

Utility Bills
Car & Health Insurance
Cell Phone Bills

The percentage of debts to income is called the debt-to-income (a.k.a. back-end) ratio.

An example of the income to debt calculation is as follows:

Income	=	$3,000
New Mortgage Payment	=	$ 900

Minimum Monthly Payments   = $ 300

"Mortgage"   /   "Income"   =   30%

"Mortgage   +   Monthly Payments"   /   "Income"   = 40%

In this scenario, your front-end is 30% and back-end is 40%, which is acceptable for many loan programs.

Always keep in mind that the higher the interest rates the higher the monthly payment. In situations where your overall monthly debt is at a level that is currently considered excessive, negotiating for a lower interest rate or paying points to buy down the interest rate may allow you to qualify for the amount of loan you desire.

DEBT TO INCOME RATIO (DTI%)

Monthly Income

Borrower   Co-Borrower
$_____ Base Pay/ _____ $_____ Base Pay/ _____
$_____ Commission/ _____ $_____ Commission/ _____
$_____ Other _____ $_____ Other _____
$_____ Other _____ $_____ Other _____

$_____ Total Monthly Income $_____ Total Monthly Income

Combined Monthly Income $_____

Monthly Debt

Borrower   Co-Borrower
$_____ House/Rent Payment $_____ House/Rent Payment
$_____ Automobile Payment $_____ Automobile Payment
$_____ Credit Card _____ $_____ Credit Card _____
$_____ Credit Card _____ $_____ Credit Card _____
$_____ Credit Card _____ $_____ Credit Card _____
$_____ Personal Loan _____ $_____ Personal Loan _____
$_____ Other_____ $_____ Other_____
$_____ Other_____ $_____ Other_____

$_____ Total Monthly Debt $_____ Total Monthly Debt

Combined Monthly Debt $_____

Take combined debt $_____ (factor each debt only once – if it is a joint debt list under the primary income earner only) and divide by the combined income $_____. The percentage _____% is your monthly debt-to-income ratio.

Figure 3:13 Debt to Income Calculation Form

When your situation exceeds normal guidelines set forth by a loan program, the loan may still be approved with compensating factors. It is your loan officer's job to make a strong case for you. They will base the case on any piece of information that reflects favorably on you. You will want to be sure to provide any positive information you have available for your loan officer to use when submitting your loan application for approval.

Some compensating factors include:

- Less than 10% increase for old rent/housing payments to the new housing expense or a decrease from the old rent/housing payments to the new housing expense

- Your excellent savings ability (as shown by savings accounts, etc)

- 3 or more months cash reserves

- Extra income that cannot be used as qualifying income

- Larger than minimum down payment

- Residual income (excess after expense) of $500 per adult and $250 per child

- Time at current residence exceeds 5 years

- Time at current employment exceeds 5 years

- Overall debt-to-income ratios below maximum guideline as set forth for that approval level

- Credit scores fall within a few points of next highest level

- A perfect mortgage or rental history proven through the credit bureau

These are only examples of the most commonly used factors. Each loan package has a different set of circumstances, it is up to you, and your loan officer to determine what can be used to make the best case to the underwriting team.

Where do I fit?
Understanding Requirements

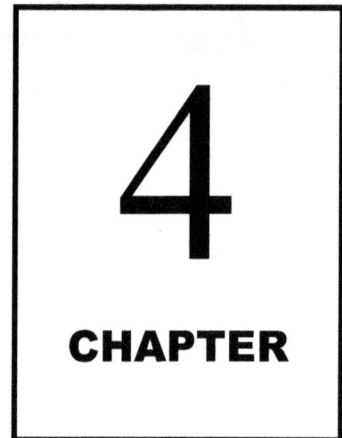

You will be required to provide documentation at the time of the loan interview and again when the final loan application is created. Sometimes another request for documentation may be made later in the loan process.

This later request will be called a stipulation list. The stipulation list is created by underwriting and is customized around your particular situation. The stipulation list is based on items the underwriter has reviewed within your profile that either raise a question in the underwriter's mind or do not fit within a specific guideline. If a piece of documentation that you submit does not fit within a specific guideline, alternate documentation will be requested. The underwriter's job is to review every item within your file to ensure that you qualify for the loan you are being offered. The purpose of underwriting guidelines is to protect the interest of the lender and minimize the risk that you will default on the loan.

The first items you should understand are the employment history and income requirements. All lenders require that you have sufficient and adequate income to cover the repayment of the mortgage. Before you can be approved for a loan, the stability of your income and continuance of income must be established through acceptable sources. Your past employment record and the employer's confirmation of continued employment must be established.

Stability of your income is generally derived from your actual employment history over the past two years. The following list shows the most common types of income seen in borrower applications and gives you a description of how you should document and use this income.

➢ A two-year employment history is needed.

➢ It is preferable that the history is in the same line of work.

➢ The actual history can be comprised of multiple jobs if necessary.

➢ Education may be included as part of the 2 year history if it was education for the same profession.

Salary or W-2 Income

You must provide documentation that shows proof that a two-year history of receiving this income exists and proof that this income is likely to continue.

The two-year history can be established by including the most recent 30-days pay stubs and the year-end W-2 for the prior two years.

Continuance of employment will be established using a V. O. E. form.

Overtime or Bonus Income

You must show proof that a two-year history of receiving this income exists.

You must also show proof that this income is likely to continue.

You will need to provide documentation, such as pay stubs for the most recent 30-day period of the present year and the final W-2 for the prior 2 years.

Each of these documents must show the inclusion of the overtime or bonus income.

The income will be factored as an average over the previous two years.

Your loan officer will request a V. O. E. from the employer confirming the history and future probability of continuance for this income.

Part-time Income
If you will use part-time income, such as income from a second job or seasonal employment, a two-year history of receiving this income must also be proven.

The documentation must show that you have a 2-year history of receiving this income without interruption

The V. O. E. will be used to show proof that the part-time income has a high probability of continuing

If the income cannot be used as qualifying income because of an interruption in receipt of the income, a lack of a two-year history or the inability to confirm the likelihood of the continuance of this income, you will still wish to document it. It may be considered as a compensating factor.

Commission Income
Commission income is based on the average of the previous 2 years income.

You must provide your full Federal Tax Returns, including all schedules, covering the past two years and you must obtain a year to date income statement from the employer.

Any un-reimbursed business expenses must be subtracted from the gross income in order to gain the usable income figures.

Retirement, Social Security, Public Assistance, or Disability Income
If you are using retirement or social security income as part of your qualification package, verification from the source of the income must be obtained.

An award letter from the social security administration or a statement of retirement income will be used for documentation purposes.

If the income will discontinue within 3 years, the income cannot be used to qualify but may be given to the loan officer as a compensating factor.

Alimony, Child Support, or Income from Separate Maintenance
This income is not required for qualification, but you may choose to use this income if you wish.

To use this income, you will need to supply a 12-month payment history from the ex-spouse or the courts showing timely payment will be required.

Evidence that such payment will continue for at least 3 years must be provided.

This evidence might be a copy of the divorce decree, settlement agreement, or other legal documents illustrating the amount of the income, history of the income, and the term for the continuance of this income.

Notes Receivable
In order to use income from a note, you must provide a copy of the endorsed and binding note.

You must also provide proof that payments have been received for a minimum of 12 months. This proof can be in the form of bank statements or copies of the cancelled payment checks.

If the note expires within 3 years, it cannot be used for qualifying but may be considered as a compensating factor.

Interest and Dividends
Interest and dividend income may be used if documentation, such as tax returns or account statements, illustrates a 2-year history or receiving this income.

Rental Income

Rent received from investment properties you own may be used if the receipt of these rents can be documented.

Income from roommates and boarders is not acceptable.

Rental income is calculated from the Schedule E of your 1040.

Depreciation can be added back in to the total received.

You should note that while positive rental income is considered as gross income, negative rental income must be treated as a recurring liability.

Copies of the leases must be provided to prove this income.

Self-Employment Income

If you own 25% or more interest in a business you can be considered self-employed.

You must have more than a one-year history for this income to be considered.

A two-year full tax return will be required.

Bank Statements

Some loan programs will allow you to use the deposits shown on 12-months or 24-months bank statements as proof of income.

In order to qualify for a bank statement program, your position must validate the probability that their business is cash based business.

The deposits showing on 12 consecutive months' bank statements will be totaled and divided by the 12 months to arrive at an average income.

Keep in mind that this is considered a light documentation loan and may be penalized with higher interest rates or a higher down payment requirement.

THIRD PARTY VERIFICATIONS

Many factors of the loan require verification of the information that you supply. This verification must be obtained from a third party who has access to specific details concerning your profile.

The following pages provide you with example forms that will be used for specific situations.

- Verification of Employment (VOE)

- Verification of Deposit (VOD)

- Verification of Rent (VOR)

- Verification of Mortgage (VOM)

Each of these verification forms will provide specific information concerning your situation, past, present and future.

The loan officer will have you sign each of these forms or a general consent to release information. They will then forward these verification forms to the appropriate company or agency for completion.

VERIFICATION OF EMPLOYMENT (VOE)

In addition to verifying your income through acceptable documentation, underwriting will often require verification of your employment and the probability of continued employment before the closing of the loan.

Verification forms will be sent to your employer to confirm all vital facts regarding employment, income, and continued employment.

A **Verification of Employment (VOE)** is a form sent to past and present employers for last two years to verify income and time on the job. Some employers have an automated 900 number for employment verification.

REQUEST FOR VERIFICATION OF EMPLOYMENT

Privacy Act Notice: This information is to be used by the agency collecting it or its assignees in determining whether you qualify as a prospective mortgagor under its program. It will not be disclosed outside the agency except as required and permitted by law. You do not have to provide this information, but if you do not your application for approval as a prospective mortgagor or borrower may be delayed or rejected. The information requested in this form is authorized by Title 38, USC. Chapter 37 (if VA); by 12 USC, Section 1701 et. Seq (if HUD/FHA); by 42 USC, Section 1452b (if HUD/CPD); and Title 42 USC, 1471 et. Seq., or 7 USC. 1971 et. Deq. (If USDA/FmHA).

Instructions   Lender – Complete items 1 through 7. Have applicant complete Item 8. Forward directly to employer named in item 1.
Employer – Please complete either Part II or Part III as applicable. Complete Part IV and return directly to lender named in item 2. This form is to be transmitted directly to the lender and is not to be transmitted through the applicant or any other party.

Part I – Request

1. To (Name and address of employer)		2. From (Name and address of Lender)	

I certify that this verification has been sent directly to the employer and ahs not passed through the hands of the applicant or any other interested party.

2. Signature of Lender	4. Title	4. Date	6. Lender's Number (Optional)

I have applied for a mortgage loan and stated that I am now or was formerly employed by you. My signature below authorizes verification of this information.

7. Name and Address of Applicant (include employee or badge number)	8. Signature of Applicant

Part II – Verification of Present Employment

9. Applicant's Date of Employment	10. Present Position	11. Probability of Continued Employment

12A. Current Gross Base Pay (enter Amount and Check Period) __ Annual __ Hourly __ Monthly __ Other (specify) $ _____ __ Weekly	13 For Military Personnel Only		14. If Overtime or Bonus is Applicable Is Its Continuance Likely? Overtime __ Yes __ No Bonus __ Yes __ No
	Pay Grade		
	Type	Monthly Amount	15. If paid hourly – average hours per week
	Base Pay	$	

Type	Year to Date	Past Year 20_	Past Year 20_	Rations	$	
Base Pay	$	$	$	Flight or Hazard	$	16. Date of applicant's next pay increase
Overtime	$	$	$	Clothing	$	17. Projected amount of next pay increase
				Quarters	$	
Commissions	$	$	$	Pro Pay	$	18. Date of applicant's last pay increase
Bonus	$	$	$	Overseas or Combat	$	19. Amount of last pay increase
Total	$	$	$	Variable Housing Allowance	$	

20. Remarks (If employee was off work for any length of time, please indicate time period and reason)

Part III Verification of Previous Employment

21. Date Hired	23. Salary/Wage at Termination Per (Year) (Month) (Week)
22. Date Terminated	Base _____ Overtime _____ Commissions _____ Bonus

24. Reason for Leaving	25. Position Held

Part IV – Authorized Signature – Federal statutes provide severe penalties for any fraud, intentional misrepresentation, or criminal connivance or conspiracy purposed to influence the issuance of any guaranty or insurance by the VA Secretary, the U.S.D.A., FmHA/FHA Commissioner, or the HUD/CPD Assistant Secretary.

26. Signature of Employer	27. Title (please print or type)	28. Date

4:1Sample Form – Verification of Employment – HUD Release

Mortgage/Rental History

Mortgage or rental history is also used to project the probability of you repaying your new mortgage as agreed. The theory behind this concept is that the manner you paid your mortgage or rent in the past predicts how responsibly you will pay the new mortgage obligation if the lender should decide to provide the funding for your new home purchase.

Mortgage histories are frequently included in a credit report. If the mortgage/rental history is not included in the credit report, it must be verified in another manner.

VOM/VOR

Verification forms sent by the loan officer or loan processor to a mortgage holder or a rental management company to verify the history of an account are called the VOR/VOM forms. This stands for verification of mortgage/verification of rent. Many lenders will not accept verification forms from a private party as these can easily be falsified. In that instance, you will need to provide alternate documentation:

> 12 months most recent cancelled rent checks or money orders

> 12 months bank statements from either you or the property owner showing 12 months concurrent withdrawals or deposits for rental

The mortgage or rental history is typically based upon the primary (owner-occupied) residence.

Mortgage histories for secondary (non-owner occupied) properties are usually calculated as consumer debt. It is important to differentiate these payments for your lender, as mortgage late payments will often effect the loan approval terms more dramatically than other late payments.

More and more lenders are placing equal or greater weights on verification of rent or mortgages payments on credit scores.

REQUEST FOR VERIFICATION OF RENT OR MORTGAGE

Instructions	Lender – Complete items 1 through 8. Have applicant complete item 9. Forward directly to landlord named in item 1.
	Landlord Creditor – Please complete Items 10 through 18 and return directly to lender named in item 2.
	This form is to be transmitted directly to the lender and is not to be transmitted through the applicant or any other party.

Part I – Request

1. To (Name and address of Landlord Creditor)	2. From (Name and address of Lender)

I certify that this verification has been sent directly to the landlord/creditor and ahs not passed through the hands of the applicant or any other interested party.

2. Signature of Lender	4. Title	4. Date	6. Lender's Number (Optional)

7. Information To Be Verified

Property Address	Account in the Name of	Account Number
	__ Mortgage __ Rental __ Land Contract	

I have applied for a mortgage loan. My signature below authorizes verification of mortgage or rent information.

8. Name and Address of Applicant(s)	9. Signature of Applicant(s)
	X
	X

Part II – To Be Completed by the Landlord/Creditor

We have received an application for a loan from the above, to which we understand you rent or have extended a loan. In addition to the information requested below, please furnish us with any information you might have that will assist us in processing the loan.

__ Rental Account	__ Mortgage Account	__ Land Contract
10. Tenant Rented from _____ to _____ Amount of rent $_____ per _____ Number of late payments _____ Is account satisfactory? __ Yes __ No	11. Date account opened _____ Original contract amount $_____ Current account balance $_____ Monthly Payment (P&I) $_____ Payment with T&I $_____ Is account current? __ Yes __ No Was loan assumed? __ Yes __ No Satisfactory account? __ Yes __ No	12. Interest Rate _____% __ Fixed __ ARM __ FHA __ VA __ CONV __ Other Next pay date _____ No. of late payments _____ No. of late charges _____ Owner of First Mortgage _____

Payment History for the previous 12 months must be provided n order to comply with secondary mortgage market requirements.

13. Additional information which may be of assistance in determination of credit worthiness

14. Signature of Landlord/Creditor Representative	15. Title (please print or type)	Date

17. Please print or type name signed in Item 14

4:2 Sample Form – Verification of Rent or Mortgage – HUD Release

SOURCE OF FUNDS FOR PURCHASES

The approval you receive will come with a LTV - Loan to Value or the amount the lender is willing to finance as opposed to the overall cost of the property and possibly a CLTV - Combined Loan to Value.

The combined loan to value is an additional amount that you may finance through subordinate financing. Subordinate financing is a second loan held by the seller of the property or an outside lending source. The balance between the LTV or CLTV and the purchase price of the property must be sourced, often as your own funds.

To source funds you must provide documentation that proves where you obtained the money toward the purchase.

You are often required to invest your own funds in the property to aid in securing the loan against default. Generally, the higher the credit risks the higher the percent of your own funds that will be required. The premise behind this requirement is that a borrower is less likely to default on a loan if they are losing their own personal funds through the default.

A loan approval with a CLTV approval amount can make a tremendous difference in the amount of money you need to buy your home.

Your cash investment in the property must be equal to the difference between the amount of the mortgage, excluding any up front fees, and the total costs to acquire the property. All funds must be verified through acceptable methods.

You should begin planning the source of funds you will need toward your down payment percentage as soon as you begin the process of shopping for a home.

Earnest Money Deposit
Upon making an offer on a property, most Real Estate Agents require you to remit an Earnest Money Deposit.

This deposit protects the agency and the seller in the event you change your mind and cancel the deal.

Once an offer has been accepted, the property is removed from the market. If you back out of a deal once the property has been removed from the market, the earnest money deposit is retained between the sellers and the real estate agent. These funds act as compensation for the loss of time involved and any costs incurred.

If you complete the transaction as planned and proceed to closing, the earnest money deposit is credited toward your purchase and closing costs.

The earnest money deposit is held in escrow, typically by the real estate agent. If the amount of earnest money exceeds 2% of the sales price or appears to be excessive based on your history of accumulating savings, the deposit amount and source of funds may require verification. Otherwise, satisfactory documentation includes a copy of your cancelled check or verification from the bank.

Savings and Checking Accounts

The lender must verify any funds that you have saved in your checking or savings account accounts. You will need to provide the most recent three months bank statements. If a large increase in deposits is present or the account was recently opened, an explanation and verification of source of funds must be established.

Non-sufficient funds, bounced checks, or overdrafts showing on the statements will need to be explained in writing.

Gift Funds

An outright gift of money toward your home purchase is usually acceptable if it is from

- a relative
- your employer
- labor union
- a charitable organization

- a governmental agency or public entity that has a program established to provide homeownership assistance to low and moderate income families.

NO REPAYMENT OF THIS GIFT MAY BE EXPECTED OR IMPLIED.

This letter must be signed by both parties and state that there is no requirement to repay the funds received.

The gift letter must

o show the dollar amount given

o be signed by the donor and the borrower

o state that no repayment is required

o show the donor's name, address, telephone number, and relationship to you

It must also contain language asserting that the funds given to you were not made available to the donor from any person or entity with an interest in the sale of the property including the seller, real estate agent, broker, builder, loan processor, or any entity associated with any of these individuals or entities.

If the gift funds are already in the your account, you must document the transfer of the funds from the donor to the yourself by obtaining a copy of the canceled check or other withdrawal document showing that the withdrawal is from the donor's personal account along with the your deposit slip or bank statement that shows the deposit.

If the gift funds are to be provided at closing by certified check, the check must be from the donors account. You must obtain a bank statement showing the withdrawal from the donor's personal account as well as a copy of the certified check. If the donor purchased a cashier's check, money order, official check or any other type of bank check as a means of transferring the gift funds, then the donor must provide a withdrawal document or canceled check for the gift showing the funds came from the donor's personal account.

If the donor borrowed the gift funds and cannot provide the documentation, the donor must provide evidence that those funds were borrowed from an acceptable source.

The donor cannot borrow the funds from a party to the transaction including the mortgage lender.

"Cash on hand" is often not an acceptable source of the donor's gift funds.

Example: A retirement account would be an acceptable source of gift funds.

There may be limitations on the amount of closing funds that may be received as a gift.

You will want to check with your loan officer to confirm the gift fund limits and ensure that the source of funds necessary does not exceed these limits.

Sales Proceeds

Sale of an asset is considered an acceptable source of income if you provide sufficient documentation. These may include:

- a copy of the bill of sale or HUD-1 Settlement Statement in the event the property is real estate

- a copy of the check or verification of transfer of funds from the buyer to your account

- a copy of your deposit slips or bank statement showing the deposit of the funds

In some cases when the value of an item is in question, you may need to prove that the sale price of the property was fair market value using appraisals, market condition proof, or other source of proof of value.

Cash saved at home (I.e.: mattress money)

Cash saved at home must be deposited in a financial institution or held by the escrow or closing agent to become an acceptable source of funds.

You must provide a written explanation of how the funds were accumulated and the length of time taken to do so. The lender must determine creditability of these savings based on your income, spending habits, and history of using financial institutions.

Many programs put a limitation on the amount of mattress money that may be used in the closing of the loan.

Rent Credit

If a portion of your current rental payment is to be used toward the purchase of the property you currently occupy, you may need to use these funds toward down payment.

You will need to provide a copy of the rental agreement showing the option to purchase and the clause stating how much of the rental payment is to be used toward the purchase. It is the lender's responsibility to show that the rent payment is above the estimated fair market rent.

Payments made in excess of the fair market rent or standard, accepted monthly rental fee for a similar property in the same area as the option property could typically be considered as your funds to close. The creative finance book in this series delves more deeply into lease option programs and the conversion methods used when obtaining conventional financing.

Seller Concession

Many loan programs have a fixed amount toward closing costs that the seller may pay on your behalf.

This amount typically ranges from 3% to 6% of the sale price of the property.

Seller's concessions must be agreed upon in the Sales Agreement to count as source of funds.

Gift Equity

If the seller of the property you are purchasing is an immediate relative like a sibling, child or parent, gift equity may be given as a seller concession toward the overall cost of the loan. This is simply a reduction in the dollar amount the seller of the property expects to receive from the sale.

The reduction is given in the form of equity rather than a monetary gift or a subordinate loan. The amount of equity that can be given as a gift between relatives is subject to maximum limitations. You will want to discuss using gift equity with your loan officer if this situation applies to you.

Gift Equity can only be given between immediate relatives.

Prepaid Charges

Any cost involved with the loan you paid in advance of closing are considered funds to close the loan. These costs could include items like the appraisal fee, application fee, or credit report fee among others.

These funds will need to be documented in the form a copy of the check written to the lender or service provider.

These are the most common source of funds acceptable to most Underwriting Teams.

This is not to be considered an all-inclusive list. You should check with your loan officer to determine any additional items that may be specific to your loan application.

Many of the sources of funds illustrated will require additional verification for documentation purposes. Some of this verification may be obtained from you. Other verification documentation must be obtained from a third party source. The most common third party verification you will encounter related to the funds that you need to close is the Verification of Deposit.

The Verification of Deposit is a form sent to your banking institutions to verify average bank account balances for past 3 months.

Some banks will charge borrower a fee of up to $20 for this verification.

REQUEST FOR VERIFICATION OF DEPOSIT

Privacy Act Notice: This information is to be used by the agency collecting it or its assignees in determining whether you qualify as a prospective mortgagor under its program. It will not be disclosed outside the agency except as required and permitted by law. You do not have to provide this information, but if you do not your application for approval as a prospective mortgagor or borrower may be delayed or rejected. The information requested in this form is authorized by Title 38, USC. Chapter 37 (if VA); by 12 USC, Section 1701 et. Seq (if HUD/FHA); by 42 USC, Section 1452b (if HUD/CPD); and Title 42 USC, 1471 et. Seq., or 7 USC. 1971 et. Deq. (if USDA/FmHA).

Instructions   Lender – Complete Items 1 through 8. Have applicant complete item 9. Forward directly to depository named in item 1.
                  Depository – Please complete Items 10 through 18 and return DIRECTLY to lender named in item 2.
                  This form is to be transmitted directly to the lender and is not to be transmitted through the applicant or any other party.

PART I - REQUEST

1. To (Name and address of depository)	2. From (Name and address of Lender)

I certify that this verification has been sent directly to the bank or depository and ahs not passed through the hands of the applicant or any other interested party.

2. Signature of Lender	4. Title	4. Date	6. Lender's Number (Optional)

7. Information To Be Verified

Type of Account	Account in Name of	Account Number	Balance
			$
			$
			$

To Depository: I/We have applied for a mortgage loan and stated in my financial statement that the balance on deposit with you is as shown above. You are authorized to verify this information and to supply the lender identified above with the information requested in Items 10 through 13. Your response is solely a matter of courtesy for which no responsibility is attached to your institution or any of your officers.

8. Name and Address of Applicant(s)	9. Signature of Applicant(s)

PART II – VERIFICATION OF DEPOSITORY To Be Completed By Depository

10. Deposit Accounts of Applicant(s)

Type of Account	Account in Name of	Account Number	Balance
			$
			$
			$

11. Loans Outstanding To Applicants

Loan Number	Date of Loan	Original Amount	Current Balance	Installments (Monthly/Quarterly)		Secured By	Number of Late Payments
		$	$	$	per		
		$	$	$	per		
		$	$	$	per		

12. Please include any additional information, which may be of assistance in determination of credit worthiness. (Please include information on loans paid-in-full in Item 11 above)

13. If the name(s) on the account(s) differ from those listed in Item 7, please supply the name(s) on the account(s) as reflected by your records.

PART III – Authorized Signature – Federal statutes provide severe penalty for any fraud, intentional misrepresentation, or criminal connivance or conspiracy purposed to influence the issuance of any guaranty or insurance by the VA Secretary, the U.S.D.A., FmHA/FHA Commissioner, or the HUD/CPD Assistant Secretary.

14. Signature of Depository Representative	15. Title (please print or type)	16. Date
17. Please print or type name signed in item 14	18. Phone No.	

4:3 Sample Form – Verification of Deposit – HUD Release

DOCUMENTATION

Depending on your specific situation, different types of documentation may be requested to support income, liabilities, proof of credit explanation and funds to close. This documentation establishes your credibility and your ability to repay the loan. While each individual case is different, following is a listing of the basic documentation required. You should gather all of the documentation that applies to your situation before going to meet with your loan officer for an application meeting.

- One full month's worth of pay stubs

- Last 2 years W-2's (salaried income) and / or last 2 years tax returns with all schedules (commission, dividend, rental income or self-employed borrowers)

- Copies of social security, pension, and/or retirement award letters (if applicable)

- Most recent three months bank statement for all accounts

- Current statements for all investment accounts

- Documentation to support funds to close

- Explanation for any credit derogatory

- Bankruptcy and discharge paperwork (if applicable)

- Divorce decree and any settlement paperwork (if applicable)

- Copies of all lease agreements for rental property (both currently owned and those leases to be obtained with the subject property being financed)

This is an all-inclusive list. You should check with your loan officer to determine any additional items that may be specific to your loan application.

Required Disclosures

The Federal Government as well as most State Governing bodies has established laws and acts that loan officers and lending institutions must follow to ensure credit is offered to all borrowers on an equal basis. These disclosure laws and regulations also ensure that you are fully informed about the loan you will receive, the criteria used to qualify you, and the overall cost or price or your loan as well as other factors that have a direct impact on your financial situation.

These laws are in place to protect your interest and to make the obtainment of housing and home mortgage funds a fair practice for all applicants.

A professional loan officer must act in an ethically sound manner and work to educate you with the knowledge that will help you to protect your financial position.

Many States have implemented minimum training requirements for mortgage loan officers. One goal of this educational training is to ensure loan officers have the necessary knowledge base to protect you, inform you, and behave in an ethical manner that complies with all federal and state statues and laws.

Not every disclosure you will receive is detailed in the coming pages. We have addressed those that require the most explanatory information. Most of the disclosures you will receive are easy to understand and self-explanatory. Those that could effect your financial decisions are the ones we have incorporated here.

The laws and regulations regarding disclosures and compliance are constantly undergoing modification and revision. The materials included in this chapter are the most up-to-date available at the time of their inclusion in this course. You should refer to the applicable Regional, State, and Federal Agencies for modifications and updates to the disclosures.

Home Mortgage Disclosure Act

The Home Mortgage Disclosure Act (HMDA) was enacted by Congress in 1975 and implemented by the Federal Reserve Board's Regulation C. This act requires lending institutions to report public loan data.

This data is used to aid in determining whether financial institutions are serving the housing needs of their communities. It is used to assist public officials in distributing public-sector investments to attract private investment to areas where it is needed. It is also used in identifying possible discriminatory lending patterns.

This regulation applies to certain financial institutions, including banks, savings associations, credit unions, and other mortgage lending institutions. Using the loan data submitted by these financial institutions, the Federal Financial Institutions Examination Council (FFIEC) creates aggregate and disclosure reports for each metropolitan area (MA). These reports are available to the public at central data depositories located in each MA.

Information that is included in the report will be gathered at the time the mortgage application is completed. Much of the information required for reports is incorporated into the 1003 application. This application will be a part of your application interview.

The personal disclosure questions asked by your loan officer are asked for this reporting purpose and the information you provide is strictly voluntary.

Fair Housing

Fair housing laws are in place to prevent discrimination against any borrower in sales, rentals, financing, or other housing related transactions. The law prohibits the discrimination against any borrower based upon race, color, national origin, religion, sex, familial status, and handicap. A recent executive order also states that practices must eliminate, to the extent possible, barriers arising from a limited proficiency in English to the use or participation in any federally conducted program and agency.

The Federal Fair Housing Act prohibits the use of discriminatory advertising or advertisements that state a preference for a particular type of person. A credit provider may not advertise in a manner meant to attract or deter a potential client based on race, color, religion, sex, handicap, familial status, or national origin.

Federal Agencies evaluate their policies and programs on a regular basis to determine any modifications and executive orders that must be added as a protected class under the fair housing laws.

Along with the Fair Housing Act, the Equal Credit Opportunity Acts establish guidelines and regulations regarding the discrimination against borrowers.

Equal Credit Opportunity Act/Fair Housing Act

The Equal Credit Opportunity Act and the Fair Housing Act ensures that all consumers are given the same opportunity to obtain credit.

What this does not mean is that an applicant who does not meet guidelines will obtain credit.

What this does mean is that all credit applicants must receive a level consideration regardless of outside factors or personal considerations.

Pre-qualification services must be provided to all borrowers equally. It is illegal to include discriminatory factors as criteria for the determination on a loan package.

The Equal Credit Opportunity Act (ECOA) and Fair Housing Act (FHA) identify a number of factors that are illegal to use in evaluating an applicant's qualifications.

Race, Color, Religion, Sex, National Origin, Marital Status, Age (provided the applicant is capable of entering a legally binding contract), Source of Income, Handicap and Familial Status.

A lender may decline an oral or written application as long as the decline is based upon legitimate underwriting standards applied to all loan packages. The denial may not be based upon one of the prohibited items listed above.

You should understand the difference between an "inquiry" and an "application". Many requirements apply only to applications. The regulations describe a loan application as:

An oral or written request for an extension of credit that is made in accordance with the procedures established by a creditor for the credit type listed.

Procedures established refer to the actual practices followed by a creditor for making credit decisions as well as its stated application procedures.

The Equal Credit Opportunity Act protects against other items beyond credit discriminatory actions. ECOA has provisions in place regarding predatory lending tactics and abusive activities with in the lending arena.

Creditors must provide you with notices of the actions taken on your credit application. These notices include approvals, counteroffers, and credit denial.

- Approval notices provide you with specific information regarding the loan program for which you have been approved.

- A counteroffer provides vital information to you in the event the loan terms are changed between the date of application and the date of closing.

    Changes between the application and closing can occur for a variety of reasons.
    For instance if you apply with one property in mind and then choose a different property with slightly different acceptance terms there will be alterations to the loan offering to conform to the new property offer.

    Changes to the loan between application and closing may also occur for less respectable reasons. A lender may alter the terms of the loan to incorporate additional income and fees in the principal borrowed. A lender offering a second mortgage may alter the terms of the loan to incorporate a refinance of the first mortgage and therefore improve their lien position and increase the loan amount funded.

    These tactics, among others, fall within the term predatory lending. These tactics are unlawful under federal lending acts.

FINANCIAL DISCRIMINATION ACT
FAIR LENIDNG NOTICE

It is illegal to discriminate based on

1. Trends, characteristics, or conditions in a neighborhood unless the financial institution is able to demonstrate that such consideration is required to ensure safety

2. Race, color, religion, sex, marital status, familial status, national origin, ancestry, or handicap

It is illegal to consider the racial, ethnic, religious, or national origin composition of a neighborhood or geographic area surrounding a housing accommodation or whether such composition is undergoing change.

These provisions govern financial assistance for the purpose of purchase, construction, rehabilitation, or refinancing of one to four unit residences occupied by the owner.

If you have any questions about your rights, or if you wish to file a complaint you may contact:

5:1 Sample Form – Financial Discrimination Act Fair Lending Notice – HUD Release

Federal Equal Credit Opportunity Act Notice

The Federal Equal Credit Opportunity Act prohibits creditors from discriminating against credit applicants on the basis of color, religion, national origin, sex, marital status, age (provided the applicant has the capacity to enter into a binding contract), because all of part of the applicant's income is derived from public assistance programs, or because the applicant has in good faith exercised any right under the Consumer Protection Act

Lending institutions are prohibited from bringing up certain specific subjects that lend themselves to discrimination. These subjects are as follows:

Whether or not an applicant has or will have children.

Whether or not there exist childcare problems.

Whether or not there will be interruptions of income due to childbirth.

Whether or not an applicant is receiving alimony, child support, or separate   maintenance unless this income is voluntarily disclosed as a source of additional   income to be considered as part of the credit application

Whether an applicant is widowed, divorced, or single

Whether or not an applicant's telephone number is publicly listed

Lending institutions must take and report actions taken on your applications within a reasonable time. If the application is denied, the reason for the denial must be provided if requested.

I/we acknowledge that we received a copy of this notice:

5:2 Sample Form – Federal Equal Credit Opportunity Act Notice – HUD Release

Credit Information Disclosure Authorization

I / We _____Borrower Name_____ , _____Co-Borrower Name_____ hereby authorize you to release to <u>Mortgage Company Name</u> information for verification purposes.

This information may include:

Employment information including past and present employers

Banking and Savings Account Records

Mortgage Loan Rating Information

Rental History Information

A consumer credit report from a credit-reporting agency

This information is for the confidential use in processing an application for a real estate loan

A copy of this authorization and applicable signature(s) may be deemed the equivalent of the original.

5:3 Sample Form – Credit Information Disclosure Authorization – HUD Release

Whenever information is gathered about you including credit reports, employment history, financial institution data, and tax return information, a release for such information gathering must be completed.

During the transaction, the loan processor, loan officer, underwriter, or other individuals involved in completing the loan process will obtain information from multiple sources that enable them to assess your creditworthiness and ability to repay the loan.

You sign a credit and information release authorization before they begin the process of collecting the applicable data.

Real Estate Settlement Procedures Act (RESPA)

The Real Estate Settlement Procedures Act (RESPA) is enforced by HUD and deals with closing costs and settlement procedures.

The purposes of RESPA are to:

- Help you in shopping for settlement services.
- Eliminate referral fees that increase the costs of certain settlement services.

RESPA requires that you receive disclosures at various times during the mortgage application and home purchase processes.

RESPA prohibits a person from giving or accepting any thing of value for referrals of settlement service business.

RESPA prohibits a person from giving or accepting any part of a charge for services that are not performed.

RESPA prohibits home sellers from requiring you to purchase title insurance from a particular company.

Required Disclosures at Application

At the time of application, mortgage brokers and/or lenders must give you:

- An information booklet that contains consumer information about settlement services. (purchase transactions only)

- A Good Faith Estimate of settlement costs. This lists the charges you are likely to pay at settlement. This is only an estimate and the actual charges may differ.

- If a lender requires you to use of a particular settlement provider, then the lender must disclose this requirement on the GFE.

- A Mortgage Servicing Disclosure Statement, which discloses to you whether the lender intends to service the loan or transfer it to another lender.

The lender must give these disclosures to you at the time of application or mail them to you within three business days of receiving the loan application.

If the lender turns down the loan within three days, then RESPA does not require the lender to provide these documents.

Disclosures Required Prior to Settlement

- An Affiliated Business Arrangement (AfBA) Disclosure is required at or before the time of referral.

    This disclosure is required if a settlement service provider involved in a RESPA covered transaction refers you to a provider with whom the referring party has an ownership or other beneficial interest.

    The disclosure must describe the business arrangement that exists between the two providers and give you an estimate of the second provider's charges.

- When a lender refers you to an attorney, credit reporting agency or real estate appraiser to represent the lender's interest in the transaction, the referring party may not require you to use the particular provider being referred.

- The HUD-1 Settlement Statement is a standard form that clearly shows all charges concerning the settlement. RESPA allows you to request to see the HUD-1 Settlement Statement one day before the actual settlement.

Disclosures Required at Settlement

- The final HUD-1 Settlement Statement that shows the actual settlement costs of the loan transaction.

- The Initial Escrow Statement that itemizes the estimated taxes, insurance premiums and other charges anticipated to be paid from the Escrow Account during the first twelve months of the loan. The lender has up to 45 days from settlement to deliver this statement.

Disclosures Required after Settlement

- An Annual Escrow Statement must be delivered to you from the loan servicer once a year. The annual Escrow account statement summarizes all escrow account deposits and payments during the service's twelve-month computation year. It also notifies you of any shortages or surpluses in the account and advises you about the course of action being taken.

- A Servicing Transfer Statement is required if the loan servicer sells or assigns the servicing rights to your loan to another loan servicer.

RATE LOCK OR FLOAT OPTION

You must complete a rate lock or float option form. This form specifies your determination as to whether you wish to lock in the offered interest rate now or wait on the chance that the interest rate will change for the better during the loan processing stage.

The upper section of the form should provide your identifying details, the property, and the loan. The form will have two areas. You should complete and sign the area that relates to their choice.

If you wish to lock in the currently offered interest rate, you will complete the RATE LOCK section of the form. The rate lock section will show the offered rate, any points associated with the obtainment of this rate, and the number of days that the rate lock offer is applicable.

You will sign and date the form to illustrate your acceptance of the offered rate and terms.

If you wish to wait to lock the rate in the hopes that the market will improve thus improving the interest rate that the lender will offer you can obtain, you will complete the DO NOT LOCK section of the form by signing and dating the applicable area.

The borrower should receive a copy of the completed rate lock form.

RATE LOCK/RATE FLOAT OPTION

Loan Amount $_____

Property Address   _____

City, State, Zip   _____

This is to certify that I DO want to exercise my interest rate lock option at this time.

A.   My guaranteed interest rate will be ____%.

B.   The total points paid at settlement will not exceed _____. This total does not include settlement costs such as title insurance, homeowners insurance, transfer taxes, etc.

C.   This agreement will end _____ days from today. This date is called the ending date.

ACKNOWLEDGEMENT

_____   _____
Signed   Date

This is to certify that I DO NOT want to exercise my interest rate lock option at this time.

A.   I understand that my lender cannot predict interest rate changes.

B.   If I want to obtain an interest rate commitment in the future, I may do so at any time up to ___ days before the closing of my mortgage loan.

C.   I understand that I must sign an interest rate lock-in agreement to obtain a guaranteed interest rate lock.

D.   I understand that it is my responsibility to advise the lender of my desire to obtain interest rate commitment.

ACKNOWLEDGEMENT

_____   _____
Signed   Date

_____   _____
Signed   Date

5:4 Sample Form– Rate Lock / Float Option – HUD Release

AFFILIATED BUSINESS ARRANGEMENT NOTICE

If the lender has a business arrangement or interest in one of the service providers associated with the loan process or closing, the lender must give you notice of this arrangement or interest. An Affiliated Business Arrangement Notice should be provided to the borrower, and a signature obtained that acknowledges the borrowers understanding of this business arrangement or interest. You should receive a copy of this notice.

Affiliated Business Arrangement Notice

This is to give you notice that _____ has a business relationship with (Describe the nature of the relationship between the referring party and the provider(s) including percentage of ownership interest, if applicable). Because of this relationship, this referral may provide a financial or other benefit.

(A.) Set forth below is the estimated charge or range of charges for the settlement services listed. You are NOT required to use the listed provider(s) as a condition for (settlement of your loan) (or) (purchase, sale or refinance of) the subject property. THERE ARE FREQUENTLY OTHER SETTLEMENT SERVICE PROVIDERS AVAILABLE WITH SIMILAR SERVICES. YOU ARE FREE TO SHOP AROUND TO DETERMINE THAT YOU ARE RECEIVING THE BEST RATE FOR THESE SERVICES.

_____

_____

(B.) Set forth below is the estimated charge or range of charges for the settlement services of an attorney, credit reporting agency, or real estate appraiser that we, as your lender, will require you to use, as a condition of your loan on this property, to represent our interests in this transaction.

_____

_____

ACKNOWLEDGMENT

I/we have read this disclosure form and understand that (referring party) is referring me/us to purchase the above described settlement service(s) and may receive a financial benefit as a result of this referral.

_____   _____

5:5 Sample Form– Affiliated Business Arrangement Notice – HUD Release

MAILING ADDRESS CONFIRMATION

The lender who provides the funds for the closing will often ask you to sign a statement confirming your mailing address and understanding of the monthly payment dictated through the mortgage and note documents. This statement will

- Detail your correspondence information

- State the monthly payment breakdown specifics including breakdown information for PMI, school and county taxes, insurance premiums and any reserves required under the mortgage agreement

- Define any mortgage servicing information known to the mortgage lender at the time of closing

- Detail the mailing address and other contact information of the mortgage lender

You will be asked to review all of the entries on this document and confirm a receipt of a copy of the statement. The mailing address and payment confirmation is a snapshot of all of the data pertaining to the loan that was included on the previous pages and it is critical that you receive a copy of this statement.

MAILING ADDRESS CONFIRMATION / PAYMENT LETTER

From:

Re: Loan #   *** IMPORTANT, PLEASE READ THROUGHOULY ***

         Property Address

To:

Dear Homeowner:

A.   All mortgage servicing correspondence will be mailed to the above referenced property address. In order to ensure proper receipt of all mortgage servicing notifications (i.e. monthly statement, Q&A booklets, etc.) please indicate the correct mailing address if it is different from the property address. The address to mail payments and the phone number
to   call for customer service are listed below.

     Please indicate (X):

     ( )   The property address is correct as referenced above and should be used for correspondence.

     ( )   The proper mailing address is: _____

                                       _____

B.   The monthly payments on the above loan are to begin on
and   will continue monthly until

     Your monthly payment will consist of the following:

```
MONTHLY PAYMENT ........................................................$_____
MMI/PMI INSRUANCE ......................................................  _____
RESERVE FOR COUNTY TAXES ........................................  _____
RESERVE FOR HAXARD INSURANCE..................................  _____
RESERVE FOR FLOOD INSURANCE.....................................  _____
RESERVE FOR CITY TAXES.................................................  _____
RESERVE FOR ANNUAL ASSESSMENT.................................  _____
RESERVE FOR SCHOOL TAXES...........................................  _____
_____................................._____
              TOTAL MONTHLY PAYMENTS......... .$_____
```

*** Please be aware that if you have an impound account, you may see a change in your initial monthly payment figure due to information available after the closing of your loan.

We engage the services of   as its servicer. You will be receiving a billing notice from   within two weeks of your loan funding.   has the right to collect your payments and this in no way affects the terms and conditions of the mortgage instruments, other than the terms directly related to the servicing of your loan. If you do not receive a payment booklet or have other questions about the servicing of your loan, please call:

MORTGAGE SERVICING TRANSFER NOTIFICATION

In today's market, mortgage-servicing rights are often bought and sold. THE REAL ESTATE SETTLEMENT PROCEDURES ACT provides certain rights regarding the servicing of the mortgage and escrow accounts.

The servicing of a mortgage loan means the continued collection of payments, management of escrow, and the handling of all post close activity relating to the mortgage loan until the loan is paid in full.

Many lenders will sell the servicing rights of a mortgage to another company after the closing of the transaction. At the closing, information pertaining to how often the mortgage lender transfers servicing rights, the handling of such a transfer, and the effects of such transfer on your account will be disclosed. It is important that you understand these documents.

If a loan is transferred to a new servicer, the loan servicer is required to notify you in writing at least 15 days before the servicing of the loan is transferred to a new servicer.

The notice must include.

- The effective date of the transfer

- The date the new servicer will begin accepting payments.

- The name, address, and toll-free or collect call telephone number for the new servicer.

- Information concerning the continuance of any optional insurance, such as mortgage life or disability insurance

- A statement that the transfer of the loan servicing does not affect any term or condition of the mortgage documents other than the terms directly related to the servicing of the loan.

- An explanation that the payment may not be treated as late during the 60-day period beginning on the effective date of the transfer if it is mistakenly sent it to the old mortgage servicer instead of the new one.

Mortgage Servicing Disclosure

NOTICE TO MORTGAGE LOAN APPLICATNS: THE RIGHT TO COLLECT YOUR MORTGAGE LOAN PAYMENTS MAY BE TRANSFERRED. FEDERAL LAW GIVES YOU CERTAIN RELATED RIGHTS. READ THIS STATEMTN AND SIGN IT ONLY IF YOU UNDERSTAND ITS CONTENTS.

Because you are applying for a mortgage loan covered by the Real Estate Settlement Procedures Act (RESPA), you have certain rights under that Federal law. This statement tells you about those rights. It also tells you what the chances are that the servicing for this loan may be transferred to a different loan servicer. "Servicing" refers to collecting your principal, interest and escrow account payments, if any. If your loan servicer changes, certain procedures must be followed. This statement generally explains those procedures.

Transfer Practices and Requirements
If the servicing of your loan is assigned, sold or transferred to a new servicer you must be given notice of that transfer. The present loan servicer must send you notice in writing of the assignment, sale, or transfer of the servicing not less than 15 days before the effective date of the transfer. The present servicer and the new servicer may combine this information in one notice so long as the notice is sent to you within 15 days before the effective date of the transfer. The 15-day period is not applicable if a notice of prospective transfer is provided to you at settlement. The law allows a delay in the time (not more than 30 days after a transfer) for servicers to notify you under certain limited circumstances, when your servicer is changed abruptly. This exception applies only if your servicer is fired for cause, is in bankruptcy proceedings, or is involved in a conservatorship or receivership initiated by a Federal Agency.

Notices must contain certain information. They must contain the effective date of the transfer of the servicing of your loan to the new servicer, the name, address and toll-free or collect call telephone number of the new servicer, and toll-free or collect call telephone numbers of a person or department for both your present servicer and your new servicer to answer your questions about the transfer of servicing. During the 60-day period following the effective date of the transfer of the loan servicing, a loan payment received by your old servicer before its due date may not be treated by the new servicer as late and a late fee may not be imposed on you.

Complaint Resolution

Section 5 of RESPA gives you certain consumer rights *whether or not your loan servicing is transferred*. If you send a qualified written request to your loan servicer concerning the servicing of your loan, your servicer must provide you with a written acknowledgement within 20 business days of receipt of your request. A "qualified written request" is a written correspondence other than notice on payment coupon or other payment medium supplied by the servicer that includes your name and account number and your reasons for the request. Not later than 60 Business Days after receiving your request, your servicer must make any appropriate corrections to your account or must provide you with a written clarification regarding any dispute. During this 60-Business Day period, your servicer may not provide any information to a consumer reporting agency concerning any overdue payment related to such period or qualified written request.

A business day is any day excluding public holidays, State or Federal, Saturday or Sunday.

Damages and Costs

Section 6 of RESPA also provides for damages and costs for individuals in circumstances where servicers are shown to have violated the requirements of that section.

Servicing Transfer Estimated by Lender

1.   The following is the best estimate of what will happen to the servicing of your loan:

        We may assign, sell, or transfer the servicing of your loan sometime while the loan is outstanding. We are able to service your loan and we <u>presently</u> intend to service your loan.

2.   For all mortgage loans that we make in the 12-month period after your mortgage loan is funded, we estimate that the percentage of mortgage loans for which we will transfer servicing is between:

        ___ and ___%

        This is only our best estimate and it is not binding. Business conditions or other circumstances may affect

3.   This is our record of transferring the servicing of mortgage loans we have made in the past:

        Year   Percentage of Loans Transferred

5:7 Sample Form – Mortgage Servicing Disclosure – HUD Release

RIGHT TO RECEIVE A COPY OF THE APPRAISAL

When an appraisal has been conducted as a part of the transaction, you have a right to obtain a copy of said appraisal if you have paid for its completion.

- The appraisal will often be delivered directly to the lender during the course of the loan process.

- The loan processor should provide instructions to you at or before the settlement meeting on how to obtain a copy of the appraisal if you desire one.

NOTICE REGARDING YOUR
UNIFORM RESIDENTIAL APPRAISAL REPORT

You are advised that you have the right, under the Equal Credit Opportunity Act, to obtain a copy of your *Uniform Residential Appraisal Report.*

If you wish a copy, please write us at the address shown below. We must hear from you no later than 90 days after we notify you about the action taken on your credit application or you withdraw your application. Please send your written request to:

In your letter, give the following information:

    Loan or application number (if known)
    Date of application
    Name(s) of loan applicant(s)
    Property address
    Current mailing address

A copy of your Uniform Residential Appraisal Report shall be mailed to you within 30 days after receipt of your request.

5:8 Sample Form – Right to Receive a Copy of Appraisal – HUD Release

RIGHT OF RECISSION/RIGHT TO CANCEL

Some transactions must include a RIGHT for you to rescind or CANCEL the loan after the closing date.

Any credit transaction, except purchase money transactions, that involve a security interest in you primary residence must provide you with the right to rescind the transaction.

RIGHT OF RECISSION LENDER RESPONSABLITY

The lender has certain responsibilities that help to protect these rights.

- Lenders are required to provide two copies of the right to cancel or rescind to you.

- The notice must be on a separate document that identifies the rescission period available to you.

- The notice must clearly disclose the fact that your primary residence will be held as a security instrument because of the transaction.

- The notice must state your right to rescind or cancel the transaction.

- The notice must state how you may exercise the right to rescind or cancel.

- The notice must designate the address of the lender or the place of business to which the rescission or cancellation must be delivered.

- You will receive a refund of all money or property provided to the lender within twenty days of delivery of the decision to rescind or cancel the transaction.

RIGHT OF RESCISSION BORROWER RESPONSIBILITY

You also have certain responsibilities with regard to the right to cancel a credit transaction.

- In order to notify the lender of the decision to rescind or cancel the transaction you must send a written notice to the lender.

- The decision must be delivered to the lender by mail, telegram or other communication available, which allows for written delivery of your signature.

- You may exercise the right to rescind or cancel the transaction until midnight on the third day of the transaction.

- When more than one borrower in a transaction has the right to rescind or cancel the exercise of the right of rescission or cancellation by one borrower shall be binding upon all borrowers.

- When you rescind or cancel the transaction the security interest resulting from the transaction becomes void.

- You will receive a refund of all money or property provided to the lender within twenty days of delivery of the decision to rescind or cancel the transaction.

- You may waive the right to rescind by completing the applicable notice.

NOTICE OF RIGHT TO CANCEL

Your Right to Cancel

You are entering a transaction that will result in a mortgage on your home. You have a legal right under Federal Law to cancel this transaction without cost until midnight of the third business day after, whichever of the following events occurs last

     (1.)   the date of the closing of the transaction

     (2.)   the date you received your Truth in Lending disclosure

     (3.)   the date you received this notice of your right to cancel

If you cancel the transaction, the mortgage is also canceled. Within 20 calendar days after we receive your notice we must take the steps necessary to reflect the fact that the mortgage on your house has been cancelled, and we must return to you any money or property you have given to us or to anyone else in connection with this transaction. You may keep any money or property we have given you until we have completed the items mentioned above, but you must return the money or property upon completion of the described actions. If it is impractical or unfair for you to return the property, you must offer its reasonable value. You may offer to return the property at your home or at the location of the property. Money must be returned to the address below. If we do not take possession of the money or property within 20 calendar days of your offer, you may keep it without further obligation.

How to Cancel

If you decide to cancel this transaction you may do so by notifying

_____

_____

You may use any written statement that is signed and dated by you and states your intention to cancel, or you may use this notice by dating and signing below. Keep one copy of this notice because it contains important information about your rights.

If you cancel by mail, you must send the notice no later than midnight of
_____, 20___ *(or midnight of the third business day following the latest of the events listed above.) If you send or deliver your written notice to cancel in some other manner, it must be delivered to the above address no later than that time.*

5:9 Sample Form –Notice of Right to Cancel – HUD Release

SETTLEMENT STATEMENT

The settlement statement is the statement that itemizes all closing costs payable at the closing or settlement meeting.

The settlement statement will contain details derived from the good faith estimate, the sales agreement, payoff and billing information, and other specific figures supplied to the closing agent's office.

You should understand the inclusions of the settlement statement so that you can determine exactly what costs you are paying. You should confirm that the numbers included match the loan that you expected to receive.

Your portion of the settlement statement should mirror the initial Good Faith Estimate.

The settlement statement is the statement that itemizes all closing costs payable at the closing or settlement meeting.

The seller's portion of the settlement statement breaks down all items on the seller's behalf. Included in the seller's portion will be:

- any liens or mortgages that must be paid to secure a clear title to the property

- any seller concession toward the buyers closing costs (as negotiated in the Sales Agreement) and any additional charges for which the seller is responsible

- any prorated items the seller has agreed to pay as negotiated in the sales agreement

- any other costs the seller has incurred that must be paid at the closing table

You will wish to review the seller's portion to ensure that any concessions, assumed loans or costs the seller has agreed to pay as part of the purchase negotiations are correctly debited from the seller and credited to your side of the settlement statement.

The settlement statement contains the final figures pertaining to the loan. It is your duty to review the settlement statement before the closing meeting. You should confirm that all of the details set forth on the settlement statement are in agreement with the loan program offered to you by the loan officer.

Page one section 100 will contain the total of all costs involved with the loan process. These will include:

- The sales price

- Any settlement charges allocated to you

- Any pro-rated taxes due from you

Section 200 will contain all amounts, which are paid on your behalf. These will include:

- Any deposit or earnest money that you paid at the time of the Sales Agreement negotiation

- Any additional deposits or payments that you made in the course of the loan processing

- The loan amount as negotiated with the lender

- Any assumed loans you are taking over from the seller

- Any seller financing as negotiated at the time of the sales agreement

- Any closing costs to be paid by the seller as negotiated at the time of the Sales Agreement

- Any additional adjustments that the Title Company has determined must be made to the finances of the package.

The figures will be calculated, taking the amount paid on your behalf and the amount due to the seller and service providers to determine the exact figure that you must bring to the closing table.

You should review the final settlement statement to confirm that all of the figures match the loan as it has been structured and that the cash to or from you match the estimate of charges on the initial good faith estimate. A very small amount of change is expected due to the pro-rata of exact charges. However, if the figures vary greatly from the initial estimate, the Settlement Statement will need to be reviewed with more care to determine exactly where the error has occurred.

Page two of the settlement statement contains a more detailed breakdown of the charges included in the section titled settlement charges to borrower. The fees and costs being charged on the loan will be included in this section. These figures will mirror the good faith estimate making an error relatively simple to find.

F. Type of Loan				
1__ FHA 2__ FmHA 3__ Conv 4__ VA 5__ Conv Ins	6. File Number:	7. Loan Number:	8. Mortgage Insurance Case Number	

G. Note: This form is furnished to give you a statement of actual settlement costs. Amounts paid to and by the settlement agent are shown. Items marked "(P&C)" were paid outside the closing; they are shown here for informational purposes and are not included in the totals.

D. Name & Address of Borrower.	E. Name & Address of Seller	F. Name & Address of Lender
G. Property Location	H. Settlement Agent Place of Settlement:	I. Settlement Date

J. Summary of Borrower's Transaction			K. Summary of Seller's Transaction		
100. Gross Amount Due From Borrower			**400. Gross Amount Due To Seller**		
101. Contract Sales Price			401. Contact Sales Price		
102. Personal Property			402. Personal Property		
103. Settlement Charges to borrower (line 1400)			403.		
104.			404.		
105.			405.		
Adjustments for items paid by seller in advance			Adjustments for items paid by seller in advance		
106. City / Town Taxes	for		406. City / Town Taxes	for	
107. County Taxes	for		407. County Taxes	for	
108. Assessments	for		408. Assessments	for	
109.			409.		
110.			410.		
111.			411.		
112.			412.		
120. Gross Amount Due From Borrower			**420. Gross Amount Due To Seller**		
200. Amounts Paid By Or In Behalf Of Borrower			**500. Reductions In Amount Due To Seller**		
201. Deposit or earnest money			501. Excess deposit (see instructions)		
202. Principal amount of new loan(s)			502. Settlement charges to seller (line 1400)		
203. Existing loan(s) take subject to			503. Existing loan(s) taken subject to		
204.			504. Payoff of first mortgage loan		
205.			505. Pay off of second mortgage loan		
206.			506.		
207.			507.		
208.			508.		
209.			509.		
Adjustments for items unpaid by seller			Adjustments for items unpaid by seller		
210. City / Town Taxes	for		510. City / Town Taxes	for	
211. County Taxes	for		511. County Taxes	for	
212. Assessments	for		512. Assessments	for	
213.			513.		
214.			514.		
215.			515.		
216.			516.		
217.			517.		
218.			518.		
219.			519.		
220. Total Paid By/For Borrower			**520. Total Reduction Amount Due Seller**		
300. Cash At Settlement From/To Borrower			**600. Cash at Settlement To/From Seller**		
301. Gross amount due from borrower (line 120)			601. Gross amount due to seller (line 420)		
302. Less amounts paid by/for borrower (line 220)	(	)	602. Less reductions in amt due seller (line 520)	(	)

5:10 Sample Form – HUD 1 Settlement Statement Page 1 – HUD Release

		Paid From Borrowers Funds at Settlement	Paid From Seller's Funds at Settlement
700. Total Sales/Brokers commission based on price $ @ %			
Division of Commission (line 700) as follows:			
701. $ to			
702. $ to			
703 Commission paid at Settlement			
704.			
800. Items Payable in Connection with Loan			
801. Loan Origination Fee %			
802. Loan Discount %			
803. Appraisal Fee to			
804. Credit Report to			
805. Lender's Inspection Fee			
806. Mortgage Insurance Application Fee to			
807. Assumption Fee			
808.			
809.			
810.			
900. Items Required By Lender To Be Paid In Advance			
901. Interest from to @$ / day			
902. Mortgage Insurance Premium for months to			
903. Hazard Insurance Premium for years to			
904.			
905.			
1000. Reserves Deposited With Lender			
1001. Hazard Insurance months @$ per month			
1002. Mortgage Insurance months @$ per month			
1003. City Property Taxes months @$ per month			
1004. County Property Taxes months @$ per month			
1005. Annual Assessments months @$ per month			
1006. months @$ per month			
1007. months @$ per month			
1100. Title Charges			
1101. Settlement or closing fee to			
1102. Abstract or title search to			
1103. Title examination to			
1104. Title insurance binder to			
1105. Document preparation to			
1106. Notary fees to			
1107. Attorney's fees to			
(includes above items numbers:)			
1108. Title Insurance to			
(includes above items numbers:)			
1109. Lender's coverage $			
1110. Owner's coverage $			
1111.			
1200. Government Recording and Transfer Charges			
1201. Recording fees: Deed $: Mortgage $: Releases $			
1202. City/county tax/stamps: Deed $: Mortgage $			
1203. State tax/stamps: Deed $: Mortgage $			
1204.			
1205.			
1300. Additional Settlement Charges			
1301. Survey to			
1302. Pest Inspection to			
1303.			
1304.			
1305.			
1400. Total Settlement Charges (enter on lines 103, Section J and 502, Section K)			

5:11 Sample Form – HUD1 Settlement Statement Page 2 – HUD Release

ESCROW ACCOUNT DISCLOSURE STATEMENT

When the loan is being structured, one element that must be considered is whether to impound property tax and insurance payments or to pay these billings yourself as they come due.

- At times, you will pay a portion of these bills each month as part of your monthly payment.

- The funds will then be placed into an escrow account until the billings become due.

- The lender then uses the payments that you made throughout the year to makes payment for these billings.

- At other times, you may agree to pay the billings as they become due.

This is known as impounding, not impounding, escrowing, or not escrowing payments.

Whichever method is chosen, a document will often be presented at closing that details the choices, handling and confirms the actions required of each party.

BORROWER(S):

PROPERTY ADDRESS:

NON IMPOUND NOTICE

I DO UNDERSTAND THAT THE LENDER FOR THIS MORTGAGE WILL NOT IMPOUND FOR REAL ESTATE TAXES AND HOMEOWNERS INSURANCE COVERAGE ON THE ABOVE REFERENCED ACCOUNT.

THE MONTHLY PAYMENT I WILL BE MAKING ONLY COVERS PRINCIPAL AND INTEREST ON THE LOAN.

I AM FULLY RESPONSIBLE TO PAY FOR REAL ESTATE TAXES AND HOMEOWNERS INSURACE POLICY PREMIUMS WHEN THEY BECOME PAYABLE.

5:12 Sample Form – Non Impound Notice – HUD Release

INITIAL ESCROW ACCOUNT DISCLOSURE STATEMENT

Borrower Name and Address	Lender's Name and Address
Loan No.	Telephone No.

___ Your mortgage payment for the coming year will be $_____ of which $_____ will be for principal and interest and $_____ will go into your escrow account.

___ Your first monthly mortgage payment for the coming year will be $_____ of which

$_____ will be for principal and interest and $_____ will go into your escrow account.

The terms of your loan may result in changes to the principal and interest payments during the year.

This is an estimate of activity in your escrow account during the coming year based on payments anticipated to be made from your account.

Month/ Payment No.	Payments to Escrow Acct.	Payment from Escrow Acct.	Description	Escrow Acct. Balance

Please keep this statement for comparison with the actual activity in your account at the end of the escrow accounting computation year. Cushion selected by the servicer is $_____.

5:13 Sample Form – Initial Escrow Account Disclosure Statement – HUD Release

PRO-RATA CALCULATIONS

The function of completing the pro-rata calculations will often be assigned to the title agent in charge of the loan file or to the closing agent who works for the mortgage lender.

Prorating allows for you and seller to split the costs and income related to the property fairly according to the terms of ownership. These prorations may be based on the date of closing or another date as negotiated within the sales contract.

Items subject to pro-rata may include

- Real estate taxes

- Homeowner's insurance premiums

- Accrued interest on assumed loans

- Rents received on income producing property

- Other income received from an income producing property

- Expenses incurred on an income producing property

- Oil or other fuel tank filling costs

- Any utility billing for any utility not turned off and paid in full prior to the date of closing

- Any other negotiated matter.

These are the most common items subject to pro ration negotiations, but as each transaction is different, the items to be pro-rated may be different. It is important that any financial matter that may be subject to a split between you and the seller be negotiated, in writing, in the sales agreement or another document. This written negotiation ensures that all parties understand the income and expenses that may be assessed. The written negotiations also provide the settlement company with the information necessary to prorate the applicable items according to the party's wishes.

30-DAY MONTH

It is customary to complete the pro ration calculations based on a 30-day month rather than altering the figures to the exact number of days within the closing month. This 30-day month is used when prorating

- Mortgage Interest

- Property Taxes

- Water Bills

- Insurance Premiums

- and other items as determined by the specific transaction.

If the use of the customary 30-day month creates a significant financial impact on either you or the seller, you can agree to prorate using the exact number of days in the applicable month or to use the 365-day year to find the daily pro ration calculation rate. Any negotiation of this sort will be incorporated into the sales contract or written as an addendum to the sales contract.

REAL ESTATE TAXES

To understand how pro-rata calculations affect the financial figures associated with the closing, we will define the figures for an example real estate property tax calculation.

Real estate property tax pro-rations are common to nearly every real estate transaction. The date basis for the calculation will depend on

- The number of times taxes are assessed per year

- The due date of each tax billing cycle

- The status of the payments of the taxes

- The period each payment covers

In some parts of the country, it is customary for property owners to receive and pay two sets of real estate taxes per year.

Regardless of the number of times payments are required, the method of prorating the tax payments will be the same. The only change that will occur will be that the final tax figures will be based on two separate sets of calculations.

To prorate taxes, you must first determine the due date of each tax payment.

- We will assume that the tax-billing period is due April 1.

You will next determine the period this billing covers.

- We will assume that the tax-billing due on April 1 is for the period of January though December 31.

The status of the payment dictates whether the seller receives tax payment reimbursement from you or if the seller is required to remit tax funds for the payment of the tax billing at the time of closing.

- We will assume the tax payment was made as required by the seller on or before the due date.

Using a closing date of May 20 and the assumptions, you would perform the calculations to determine the monthly and daily tax rate by taking the total of the yearly taxes. In our example the

> Yearly Taxes total $585.00. You will divide this total figure by 12 months to determine the monthly tax costs of the property. In our example that total is $48.75 per month

$585.00   /   12   = $48.75 per month

> We have determined that the Monthly Taxes equal $48.75. Since we are using a 30-day month, we will divide the monthly figure by 30 to determine that the daily tax rate equals $1.625.

$ 48.75   /   30   = $ 1.625 daily rate

> The Seller Portion of the taxes covers the period of January 1 though May   20.

You will take the $48.75 monthly figure and multiply it by the four months allocated to the seller to total $195.00.

$48.75   x   4   = $195.00

You will then take the $1.625 daily figure and multiply it by the 20 extra days allocated to the seller to total $32.50.

$ 1.625   x   20   = $ 32.50

You will add the total of the monthly calculations and the daily calculations to determine that the total taxes assessed to the seller equals $227.50.

$195.00   +   32.50 = $227.50

➢   This example leaves your portion of the taxes to cover the period of May 21 through December 31.

You have the baseline figures for both the monthly and daily tax rate from your seller allocation calculations.

You will use again use the $48.75 monthly figure but this time you multiply it by the 7 months allocated to you. The monthly total allocated to you equals 341.25.

$48.75   x   7   = $341.25

You will then take the daily figure of 1.625 and multiply it by the 10 days remaining in the month. 10 days plus the 20 days already accounted for on the sellers side equals the 30-day month. This calculation example has you paying $16.25 to cover the daily allocation of the taxes.

$ 1.625   x   10   = $ 16.25

You will then add the $341.25 monthly figure to the $16.25 daily figure to determine that the total taxes that you will owe equals $357.50.

$341.25   + $16.25   = $357.50

➢   You may confirm that your calculations are correct by adding your portion and the seller portion and then comparing it to the total taxes due on the property.

If the tax payments are due twice yearly, you will calculate the second payment in the same manner and add both figures to achieve a total allocation of the taxes.

The figures will be entered as either a positive or a negative on the good faith estimate depending on the status of the payment.

> ➤ In other words, payment for the taxes due has been made by the seller, you will repay the seller for their portion at the settlement table.

> ➤ If taxes due have not been paid by the seller, the sellers tax portion will be given back to you to pay the taxing authority as part of the settlement process.

This figure can be entered as a positive figure on the good faith estimate.

HAZARD INSURANCE

Hazard insurance is typically paid in advance based on the billing received from the hazard insurance company providing the coverage. At the beginning of each year of the policy, the premium for that year's coverage must be paid. At times, a billing cycle such as monthly or quarterly payments may be negotiated with the insurance company. When real estate is sold, you may ask the seller to transfer the current insurance coverage or you may obtain new coverage through the insurance company of your choice. If the existing coverage is transferred, the premiums required will be allocated to you and seller respectively based upon the date of the closing or other date as negotiated in the sales contract.

You will need to obtain information pertaining to the insurance coverage to begin the process of prorating the premiums. This might include:

- The frequency of payment for the policy

- The total premium of the policy

- The exact term covered by the policy premium

    Example: A payment is made one time of year.

                    The total premium is $660 per coverage period.

                    The coverage period extends from November 1 to October 31.

                    The sales contract negotiates that:

- you will assume the sellers insurance policy from the date of closing

- closing is held on May 1

                    Both you and the seller will be responsible for 50% of the total premium.

                    The seller has paid the premium in full in advance

                    You owe the seller exactly $330 for the insurance coverage

Truth-In-Lending Act Regulation Z

The Truth-in-Lending act (TILA) is a part of the Consumer Credit Protection Act. TILA is meant to protect and inform you by requiring disclosures regarding loan terms and costs. This regulation applies to all institutions offering credit.

- TILA allows you to compare the cost of cash transactions against the costs of a credit transaction.

- TILA also provides an easy to understand format for you when comparing one lending institutions terms against those of another lending institution.

The regulations require lenders to:

- Disclose the maximum, potential interest rate for all variable rate transactions

- Limit home equity plans that incorporate the costs of financing in the principal balance of the loan.

- Adhere to disclosure standards for advertisement that refer to credit terms

- Provide you with fair rights of rescission.

The specific disclosures you will receive include:

- ARM Loan disclosure

- Right of rescission notice

- Advertising practice disclosures

TILA also requires that lenders make certain disclosures concerning RESPA. These disclosures must be provided with in three days of an application for credit. The initial disclosures will be partially based upon information provided by you to the loan officer. A final series of disclosures will be provided at the time of settlement that contains the confirmed and final information regarding the loan and loan terms.

DEFINITION OF TRUTH-IN-LENDING TERMS

ANNUAL PERCENTAGE RATE

This is not the note rate (the quoted interest rate) for which you applied. The Annual Percentage Rate (APR) is the cost of the loan in percentage terms. The APR takes into account a variety of loan charges; interest is only one of these charges. Other charges, which are used in the calculation of the APR, are PMI (when applicable) and any Prepaid Finance Charges (loan discount, origination fees, prepaid interest and any other credit costs added to the loan package). The APR is calculated by spreading the cost of these charges over the life of the loan. This often results in a higher rate than the interest rate shown on the Mortgage/Deed of Trust Note. If interest were the only Finance Charge, the interest rate and the APR would be the same.

PREPAID FINANCE CHARGES

Prepaid Finance Charges are charges that must be paid at the closing of the loan. The Federal Reserve Board Regulation Z defines these charges. You must pay these charges. Some examples of the charges are origination fee, discount fee, PMI, and tax service fee. Some loan charges are excluded from the Prepaid Finance Charges such as appraisal fees and credit report fees.

FINANCE CHARGE

The amount of interest, prepaid finance charges and certain insurance premiums (when applicable) that you are expected to pay over the life of the loan.

AMOUNT FINANCED

The Amount Financed is the loan amount you have applied to borrow less any prepaid finance charges. The prepaid finance charges are found on the Good Faith Estimate. For example, if your note is for $100,000 and the prepaid finance charges are $5,000 then the amount financed is equal to $95,000. The Amount Financed is the amount on which the APR is based.

TOTAL OF PAYMENTS

This figure represents the total of all of the payments that will be made toward principal, interest and mortgage insurance (when applicable) over the life of the loan.

PAYMENT SCHEDULE

The figure represented in the Payment Schedule are the principal and interest, plus PMI (when applicable) over the life of the loan. These figures do not reflect taxes and insurance escrows or any buy down payments that were contributed by the seller.

5:14 Definition of Truth in Lending Terms

Adjustable Rate Mortgage Disclosure

If your primary dwelling is going to be secured by an Adjustable Rate or Variable Rate loan, TILA requires additional disclosures to be provided with regard to the Adjustable Rate Mortgage.

The loan officer must provide you with:

- The Consumer Handbook on Adjustable Rate Mortgages

  The Federal Home Loan Bank Board publishes this handbook.

- A disclosure for each variable rate program offered to you

- The disclosures must contain all the necessary information required by Regulation Z

ADJUSTABLE RATE MORTGAGE DISCLOSURE STATEMENT

IMPORTANT MORTGAGE LOAN INFORMATION - PLEASE READ CAREFULLY

PROGRAM NAME: _____

You have expressed an interest in applying for an Adjustable Rate Mortgage loan (ARM). This disclosure contains information regarding the differences between this ARM and other mortgage loans. This disclosure describes the features of the specific ARM that you are considering. Upon request, we will provide you with information about any other Adjustable Rate Mortgage programs we have available.

ADJUSTABLE RATE MORTGAGE LOAN: This loan is an Adjustable Rate Mortgage loan. The interest rate may change based upon movements of a specific interest rate index. Changes in the interest rate will be reflected by increases or decreases for payments. The date or dates on which changes can occur will be specified in the ARM loan documents. This ARM is based on the terms and conditions of the program in which you have expressed an interest. We have based this disclosure on recent interest rates, index and margin values, and fees.

THIS DISCLOSURE: This disclosure is not a contract or loan commitment. The matters discussed in this disclosure are subject to change by us at any time without notice. DETERMINING THE INTEREST RATE: Your interest rate will be determined by means of an index that is subject to change.

Your interest rate is based on the Index value plus a margin. A change in the index generally will result in a change in the interest rate. If the Index rate change since the previous adjustment is less than _____, the interest rate will not change. The amount that your interest rate change may also be affected by periodic interest rate change limitations and the lifetime interest rate limits set forth in your loan program.

Interest Rate Adjustments Your interest rate under this ARM can change every _____ years.

Your interest rate cannot increase or decrease more than ____ percentage points at each adjustment.

Your interest rate cannot increase or decrease more than ____percentage points over the term of your loan.

Rate adjustments under this ARM will be reflected in higher or lower payments.

DETERMINING THE PAYMENTS: Your initial monthly payment of principal and interest will be determined based on the interest rate, loan term, and loan balance when your loan is closed. Your payment will be set to amortize the loan over a period of ___ payments.

Frequency of Payment Changes: Based on increases or decreases in the Index, payment amounts under this ARM loan can change every ____ years. Your monthly payment amount could change more frequently if there is a change in other loan factors not relating to the ARM. These factors may include taxes, assessments, insurance premiums, or other charges required when creating an escrow or impound account.

Limitations on Payment Changes: Your payment can change every ___ years based on changes in the interest rate, loan term, or loan balance.

Adjustment Notices: You will be notified if interest rate changes occur. If an interest rate change effects your monthly payment, you will be notified at least 25 calendar days before the changed payment is due. The notice will indicate the adjusted payment amount, interest rate, Index value, and the outstanding loan balance at that time.

** INSERT AN EXAMPLE AND INDEX TABLES AS THEY APPLY TO THE ARM UNDER DISCUSSION.

I/we acknowledge that we have received a copy of this disclosure:

5:15 Sample Form –ARM Disclosure – HUD Release

Homeownership Equity Protection Act (HOEPA)

The homeownership equity protection of 1994 is designed to protect you against unfair and abusive lending tactics. This act was created as an amendment to the Truth-in- Lending Act (TILA) Regulation Z.

HOEPA establishes requirements regarding interest rates and fees. The loans covered under HOEPA include:

- First mortgage transactions where the APR exceeds 8% of the current prime rate as established by the Treasury securities of comparable maturity

- Second mortgage transactions in which the APR exceeds 10% of the current prime rate as established by the Treasury securities index of comparable maturity

- Loans where the total fees and points paid by you exceed 8% of the total loan amount or the fixed figure established yearly. The greater of the two costs is used to establish requirements.

The loans affected are generally termed high rate or high fee loans. This type of loan is seen more frequently within the sub-prime industry than the prime industry.

The Act does not include provisions regarding construction loans, reverse mortgage transactions, or equity lines of credit.

You will receive specific disclosures regarding the loan terms and fees:

- Right to cancel

- Specific information regarding APR, monthly payment amounts, and the loan amount

- Variable rate or Adjustable rate mortgages require an additional disclosure that states the monthly payment and the interest rate are subject to change. The disclosure must state the maximum amount of change that may occur.

Homeowners Protection Act of 1998

In 1998, additional homeowner's protection regulations were put into place. These regulations are designed to assist you in understanding and minimizing the private mortgage insurance costs accrued.

Private mortgage insurance is used to allow more individuals to purchase homes with a minimal amount of cash down payment. Most lenders require PMI until you obtain an equity position in the home of greater than 20%. PMI benefits you in that the placement of the insurance enables you to obtain home financing without a large cash down payment.

PMI requirements can be removed if you are able to pay 20% of the sales price in down payment. Since most borrowers are unable to provide 20% of the sales price in cash at the time of closing, purchasing the PMI policy enables the lender to provide financing while minimizing risk.

Once you reach an equity position of 20% of the property value PMI premiums are no longer needed to protect the position of the lender. At this point, you are no longer required to continue making yearly premium payments. Unfortunately, PMI has proven difficult to cancel in the past.

Regulations are now in place that outlines the cancellation requirements and the processes for cancellation.

Borrower Initiated Cancellation

The Homeowner Protection Act of 1998 provides remedies for cancellation of the PMI coverage and an end to the yearly premium payments. If you obtain a 20% equity position in the property and have a good payment history on your loan, you may request that your PMI be cancelled. For you to initiate a cancellation request:

- The loan must have reached an 80% LTV based upon the initial amortization schedule provided to you. Adjustable rate mortgages are based on Adjustable Amortization Schedules.

- You must have a good payment history. No mortgage payments may have been more than 60 days late with in the preceding 24-month period or no mortgage payments more than 30 days late within the proceeding 12-month period.

- The mortgage holder approves the valuation of the property through verified methods such as appraised value.

- The equity position must be free and clear. No subordinate liens may be held against the equity position of 20%.

Automatic Cancellation

- HOEPA also requires that the PMI be automatically cancelled when your equity position reaches 22%.

- When a mortgage that is subject to PMI reaches a 78% LTV based upon the initial amortization schedule, the PMI must be automatically terminated if you are current on mortgage payment obligations.

- If you are not current on mortgage payment obligations, the PMI must be terminated when you bring your balance current.

High-Risk Mortgages

HOEPA bases the determination of a high-risk loan on the guidelines defined by Fannie and Freddie. The PMI payments on a high-risk loan are automatically terminated when the loan reaches a 77% loan to value or the term reaches half-life. The cancellation is based upon whichever level occurs first.

PRIVATE MORTGAGE INSURANCE INITIAL DISCLOSURE

Borrower:_____ Co-Borrower:_____

Property Address:_____

PRIVATE MORTGAGE INSURANCE TERMINATION DISCLOSURE

We SAMPLE MORTGAGE COMPANY require that you BORROWER NAME maintain private mortgage insurance ("PMI") in connection with your mortgage loan. PMI protects lenders and others against financial loss in case of borrower default. Federal law provides you with the right to cancel PMI under certain circumstances. Federal law establishes when PMI must be terminated. This Disclosure describes those cancellation and termination rights.

___1.   We have provided you with an initial amortization schedule. Federal Law basis the cancellation and termination terms on this initial amortization schedule.

___2.   Borrower Initiated Cancellation: A borrower may initiate cancellation if certain requirements are satisfied.

Term Requirements of Cancellation:

You have the right to request cancellation of PMI at any time on or after:

The date that the principal balance of the loan, based on the initial amortization schedule, reaches 80% of the original value (lesser of sales price or appraised value) of the property securing the loan.

the   The date that the principal balance of the loan, based on actual payments made, reaches 80% of the original value (lesser of sales price or appraised value) of the property securing the loan.

Status Requirements for Cancellation:

PMI may be cancelled when you reach the stated percentage if you meet all of the following requirements:

You must submit your cancellation request in writing to the servicer of your loan.

You must have a good payment history on your loan.

past   A good payment history is described as a history where you have not made a mortgage payment that was 60 days or longer due during the 24 months preceding the cancellation date.

past   The description of a good payment history also requires you have not made a mortgage payment that was 30 days or longer due during the 12 months proceeding the cancellation date.

You must have provided the note holder with

Evidence that the value of the property securing the not has not declined below its original value

Certification that you do not have a subordinate lien on the equity in the property

___3.   Automatic Termination: If mortgage loan payments are current, PMI will automatically terminate when the principal balance of the loan is scheduled to reach 78% of the original value (lesser of sales price or appraised value) of the property based on the initial amortization schedule.

The loan servicer will notify you when the automatic cancellation of PMI occurs.

___4.   Exemptions

There are certain exemptions to the right to cancellation and automatic termination of PMI. These exemptions relate to certain mortgage loans with higher risks associated with the extension of credit. These exemptions do not apply to your loan transaction.

I/We have received a copy of this Private Mortgage Insurance Termination Disclosure.

CLOSING COSTS

The good faith estimate of settlement charges allows you to be prepared for the costs involved with the closing of the loan. The initial good faith estimate will mirror your settlement statement.

The settlement statement or HUD 1 is the final accounting of costs and charges on your loan package. A slight variation between the initial good faith estimate and the final Settlement Statement may be expected due to the final pro-ratio of the taxes and specific service provider billing. If there is a large variation between the costs disclosed on the Good Faith Estimate and the Settlement Statement, you will want to compare the documents carefully and contact your loan officer to determine where the discrepancy occurred.

Regulations allow you to request a copy of your settlement statement 24-hours before closing. It is recommended that you do so to ensure your costs are as expected.

Many of the costs involved in closing a loan are standard in the industry or in the region. Items such as appraisal fee, pest inspections, and Title Search will be relatively standard.

Your funding source will require other payments. These items are specific to the funding source and may vary among lenders. You will want to discuss with your loan officer what fees their office requires.

Other costs are part of the loan officer's payment or commission package.

In general, your closing costs will be structured toward the type of loan that you are receiving.

While we are explaining to you the purpose of the various fees and costs, you should always keep in mind when negotiating closing costs that each person who works on your loan will need to be paid. Most loan officers are commission only, in other words, they only receive the payment you pay on the loan and do not receive a salary for their work. It is unrealistic to expect the loan officer to work for absolutely nothing. However, the closing costs should be fair and reasonable.

Pay close attention to the disclosed closing costs before agreeing to the financing offered. Different lenders will offer a different closing cost package. You must expect the loan officer to receive compensation for their efforts. It is important that you understand the various ways that you can provide this payment for the services you receive.

If you are cash poor, you may want to pay a slightly higher interest rate and fewer up-front costs. In that scenario, the loan officer is paid by the difference in interest rate. If you are payment sensitive, you may wish to pay a one-time up-front commission to your loan officer and keep your interest rate lower. Discuss payment with your loan officer to determine which method will work best for you.

Lender:		Sales Price:
Address:		Base Loan Amount:
		Total Loan Amount:
Applicant(s):		Interest Rate:
		Type of Loan:
Property Address:		Preparation Date:
		Loan Number

The information provided below reflects estimates of the charges, which you are likely to incur at the settlement of your loan. The fees listed are estimates – actual charges may be more or less. Your transaction may not involve a fee for every item listed. THE NUMBERS LISTED BESIDE THE ESTIMATES GENERALLY CORRESPOND TO THE NUMBERED LINES CONTAINED THE HUD-1 OR HUD-1A SETTLEMENT STATEMENT WHICH YOU WILL BE RECEIVEING AT THE SETTLEMENT. THE HUD-1 OR HUD-1A SETTLEMENT STATEMENT WILL SHOW YOU THE ACTUAL COST FOR ITEMS PAID AT SETTLEMENT.

800	ITEMS PAYABLE IN CONNECTION WITH LOAN;		1100	TITLE CHARGES	
801	Origination Fee @ % + $	$_____	1101	Closing or Escrow Fee	$_____
802	Discount Fee @ %+$	$_____	1102	Abstract or Title Search	$_____
803	Appraisal Fee	$_____	1103	Title Examination	$_____
804	Credit Report	$_____	1105	Document Preparation Fee	$_____
805	Lender's Inspection Fee	$_____	1106	Notary Fee	$_____
806	Mortgage Insurance Fee	$_____	1107	Attorney's Fee	$_____
807	Assumption Fee	$_____	1108	Title Insurance	$_____
808	Mortgage Broker Fee	$_____			$_____
810	Tax Related Service Fee	$_____			$_____
811	Application Fee	$_____			$_____
812	Commitment Fee	$_____			$_____
813	Lender's Rate Lock-In Fee	$_____			$_____
814	Processing Fee	$_____			$_____
815	Underwriting Fee	$_____			$_____
816	Wire Transfer Fee	$_____			$_____

900	ITEMS TO BE PAI DIN ADVANCE ;		1200	GOVERNMENT RECORDING AND TRANSFER CHARGES	
901	Interest for 1 days @ $13.78 day	$_____	1201	Recording Fee	$_____
902	Mortgage Insurance Premium	$_____	1202	City/County Tax/Stamps	$_____
903	Hazard Insurance Premium	$_____	1203	State Tax/Stamps	$_____
904	County Property Taxes	$_____	1205	Intangible Tax	$_____
905	Flood Insurance	$_____			$_____
		$_____			$_____

1000	RESERVES DEPOSITED WITH LENDER		1300	ADDITIONAL SETTLEMENT CHARGES	
1001	Hazard Ins 3 Mo @ $ 35 Per Mo $_____		1201	Survey	$_____
1002	Mortgage Ins. Mo@$ Per Mo $_____		1202	Pest Inspection	$_____
1004	Tax & Assmt. 7 Mo@$110 Per Mo $_____		1203		$_____
1006	Flood Insurance	$_____	1205		$_____
		$_____		TOTAL ESTIMATED SETTLMENT CHARGES $_____	

S/B designates these costs to be paid by Seller / Broker   A designates those costs effecting APR

TOTAL ESTIMATED MONTHLY PAYMENT		TOTAL ESTIMATED FUNDS TO CLOSE	
Principal & Interest	$_____	Real Estate Taxes	$_____
Down Payment	$_____	Hazard Insurance	$_____
Estimated Closing Costs	$_____	Flood Insurance	$_____
Estimated Prepaid Items	$_____		
Mortgage Insurance	$_____	Total Paid Items (subtract)	$_____
Other	$_____	Other	$_____
TOTAL MONTHLY PAYMENT $_____		CASH FROM BORROWER	$_____

The first section of the good faith estimate will define items that are payable in connection with the obtainment of the loan.

800	ITEMS PAYABLE IN CONNECTION WITH LOAN;		
801	Origination Fee @	% + $	$_____
802	Discount Fee @	% + $	$_____
803	Appraisal Fee		$_____
804	Credit Report		$_____
805	Lender's Inspection Fee		$_____
806	Mortgage Insurance Application Fee		$_____
807	Assumption Fee		$_____
808	Mortgage Broker Fee		$_____
810	Tax Related Service Fee		$_____
811	Application Fee		$_____
812	Commitment Fee		$_____
813	Lender's Rate Lock-In Fee		$_____
814	Processing Fee		$_____
815	Underwriting Fee		$_____
816	Wire Transfer Fee		$_____

6:2 Sample Form Extraction – Good Faith Estimate – HUD Release

800.   ITEMS PAYABLE IN CONNECTION WITH THE LOAN

801.   Origination Fee
fee

The Origination Fee is usually known as a loan origination but is sometimes called a "point" or "points".

The origination fee covers the lenders administrative costs in processing the loan.

Often this fee is expressed as a percentage of the loan.

Generally, you pay these fees. If you and the seller negotiate a different method of payment, it will be defined within the sales agreement.

These points are charged on behalf of loan officer or

lender. There will be a limit on the number of points that the lender is allowed to charge.

They may charge points in two ways.

The first method of charging a point is to wrap the points into the interest rate that you are offered. This will be discussed further in "pricing the loan".

The second method of charging points is as an up-front fee during the closing. Any up-front points will be reflected on the good faith estimate.

A point is 1% of the loan amount.

802	Discount Fee	A discount fee is also called a loan discount point. A loan discount is a one-time charge imposed by the lender or broker to lower the rate at which the lender or broker would otherwise offer the loan.

This fee may vary.

In effect, you are paying up front to reduce the overall monthly debt related to the loan. You may use the application of a discount fee to reduce the interest rate on a loan if the monthly payment exceeds the D. T. I. Ratio and the necessary funds are available to pay the discount fee.

These fees are paid to the lender.

803	Appraisal Fee	The Appraisal Fee covers the cost of the Appraisal.

The amount the appraisal fee is set by the appraisal company.

These funds are paid to the Appraisal Company.

804	Credit Report	Any costs associated with the completion of the Credit Report will be disclosed on the good faith estimate.

Many lenders or brokers require the credit report charges be paid on all closed loans.

This amount is paid as a reimbursement to the lender.

At times, a lender may require the credit report fee be paid at the application meeting.

| 805 | Lender's Inspection | If the lender requires an inspection of the property for Underwriting purposes or another reason, the costs are your responsibility. |

| 806 | Mortgage Insurance Application Fee | If Mortgage Insurance is necessary for the loan, any associated Application Fee should be included in the good faith estimate. This fee covers the processing of an application for mortgage insurance. |

| 807 | Assumption Fee | If a loan is being assumed from the seller of the property, the lender assigning the loan to you may charge an Assumption Fee.

This fee is charged when a buyer "assumes" or takes over the duty to pay the seller's existing mortgage loan |

| 808 | Mortgage Broker Fee | Some states or specific funding lenders require that all fees charged by the Broker be differentiated on the good faith estimate. Mortgage Broker Fees are categorized with in this section of the good faith estimate.

This separate disclosure helps to differentiate the costs you are paying to the lending entity and the costs that they are paying for the brokerage services. |

| 810. | Tax Service Fee | Some lenders will use a service to verify the tax payment status of the property. Other lenders will rely on the settlement and closing company to perform this verification activity.

If a separate tax service entity is used to obtain the tax payment amounts and payment status, they will charge a fee for completing this action. The amount of the fee will vary by Service Company. |

| 811 | Application Fee | Some lenders or mortgage brokerage offices charge an up-front application fee. |

This amount may include the credit report charges, appraisal fee, or additional costs as determined by the branch location.

- Often these charges are credited toward the closing in the event the loan is completed.

- These payments are typically kept to offset any costs incurred by the branch in the event the loan does not close.

The decision to charge an application fee is determined by a particular branch location or lender. You will want to verify whether you will have to pay an application fee, the amount of the fee, and how the fee will be allocated at loan closing.

812 Commitment Fee   Some lenders or brokerages charge a Commitment Fee

This is often termed a "junk fee".

This is a fee charged by the lender in addition to points.

These fees are sometimes split per the negotiated commission schedule with the loan processor or loan officer.

813 Lender's Lock Rate Fee Some lenders will charge a specific fee for the task of locking the interest rate. This fee could be a service charge or may be a fee associated with the obtainment of a specific rate.
This fee is different from the discount points paid to buy down the interest rate.

814 Processing Fee   Some lenders or brokerages may charge a Processing Fee

This is often termed a "junk fee".

This is a fee charged by the lender in addition to points.

815 Underwriting Fee   Some lenders or brokerages charge an Underwriting Fee.

This is often termed a "junk fee".

This is a fee charged by the lender in addition to points.

These fees are sometimes split per the negotiated commission schedule with the loan underwriter, loan officer, or loan processor but are more frequently credited entirely to the lender.

816   Wire Transfer Fee

Some lenders may charge a Wire Transfer Fee to cover the costs of wiring the required funds to close the loan.

This fee is a "buyer non-allowable fee" under some program guidelines. If a wire transfer fee is being charged on behalf of the branch or lender, it will appear on the good faith estimate.

900	ITEMS TO BE PAI DIN ADVANCE	
901	Interest for days @ $ /day	$_____
902	Mortgage Insurance Premium	$_____
903	Hazard Insurance Premium	$_____
904	County Property Taxes	$_____
905	Flood Insurance	$_____

6:3 Sample Form Extraction – Good Faith Estimate – HUD Release

900   ITEMS REQUIRED BY THE LENDER TO BE PAID IN ADVANCE

Some fees related to the closing are recurring fees. These fees relate to costs associated with the carrying of the loan. The lender may require you to pre-pay a specific quantity of these recurring fees as a condition of the loan closing. Some of these items would be accrued interest, mortgage insurance premiums, and homeowner's hazard insurance.

901   Interest

Most lenders require you to pay the interest that accrues from the date of settlement or closing to the date that you will make the first monthly payment

This interest is prorated daily and based on the new loans interest rate.

902   Mortgage Insurance

	Premium	If mortgage insurance is a requirement of the loan being obtained, an up-front Premium may be charged. This premium may also be financed into the loan amount.
		If you pay the insured loan off within the first seven years, you may be entitled to a prorated refund of the fee.
903	Hazard Insurance	Hazard insurance protects you and the lender against loss due to fire, windstorm, and other hazards. Lenders often require you to bring a paid-up first year's hazard insurance policy to the settlement or to pay for the first year's premium at settlement.
904	City Property Taxes	The city where the property is located may charge property taxes on real estate. The costs will be prorated between you and the seller based on the closing date of the property and the negotiations included on the sales agreement.
905	Flood Insurance	If the lender requires flood insurance as a condition of the loan, it is usually listed within the segment of the good faith estimate relating to items to be paid in advance. Many lenders will require that you bring a fully paid policy illustrating flood coverage for the first year of homeownership as a condition of loan closing.
1004	County Property Tax	The County will assess property taxes on real estate.
		The amount of property taxes collected will vary depending on the date of closing, billing cycle of the taxes, and negotiations between you and the seller.
		The lender may require that you escrow property taxes. Escrowing taxes means that you pay a portion of the expected tax billing to the lender each month. The lender or servicer then holds these payments until the tax billing becomes due. The lender or servicer then uses the funds paid to pay the tax bills related to the property.

1100 TITLE CHARGES	
1101 Closing or Escrow Fee	$_____
1102 Abstract or Title Search	$_____
1103 Title Examination	$_____
1105 Document Preparation Fee	$_____
1106 Notary Fee	$_____
1107 Attorney's Fee	$_____
1108 Title Insurance	$_____

6:4 Sample Form Extraction – Good Faith Estimate – HUD Release

1000   TITLE CHARGES

Any costs or charges associated with securing a clear title to the property and closing of the loan will be incorporated into the good faith estimate. Although these are not lender fees, lenders must provide a quote of the estimated costs of these items and services. These quotes may vary significantly. Title charges may cover a variety of services performed by title companies and others.

1101   Closing/Escrow Fee   A Closing or Escrow Fee is paid to the settlement agent or escrow holder.

Responsibility for the payment of this fee should be negotiated between you and the seller. This negotiation will appear on the sales agreement provided to you by the real estate agent.

1102   Abstract/Title Search   Any fees required for the completion of the Abstract or Title Search on the property will be charged to you by the Title Company.

The payment of these fees may be negotiated as part of the sales agreement between you and the seller.

You can contact the closing company handling the settlement to obtain a figure for this field.

1105   Document Preparation Fee   Any cost charged by the title company for the service of preparing all of the closing documents not provided by the funding company will be entered into the good faith estimate under Document Preparation Fee.

Lender or Funding Company charges for document preparation costs will be included within a different section of the good faith estimate.

1106   Notary Fee

The charge incurred for the notary who verifies the signatures of all parties on the documents during the closing should be included within the good faith estimate.

You can contact the closing company handling the settlement to obtain a figure for this field.

1107   Attorney's Fee

In the event that the services of an attorney are required during any portion of the loan application, processing, or closing activity, the costs charged by the attorney for these services should be entered into the good faith estimate.

The attorney will provide you with an estimate of his or her charges for the requested services.

1200 GOVERNMENT RECORDING AND TRANSFER CHARGES	
1201 Recording Fee	$_____
1202 City/County Tax/Stamps	$_____
1203 State Tax/Stamps	$_____
1205 Intangible Tax	$_____

6:5 Sample Form Extraction – Good Faith Estimate – HUD Release

1200   GOVERNMENT RECORDING AND TRANSFER

Fees charged at the courthouse where the mortgage documents are filed will be allocated in association with the loan. You typically pay these costs, but you can negotiate the payment of these fees with the seller. These fees are payable to the government.

1201   Recording fee

A recording fee is the amount charged for the recording of each item that must be filed within the public records system.
These items are filed for the protection of you and the lender.

Recording costs vary depending on the region where the recording will occur. You will want to verify the costs with your Title Company, courthouse, or loan officer

1202	City/County Tax Stamps	City and County Taxes and Stamps are the taxes assessed when real property is transferred within a city and county.
		Different areas have different tax costs. You will want to verify this figure with your Title Company, courthouse, or loan officer.
1203	State Tax Stamps	State Tax Stamps are the state required taxes involved with the transfer of the property.
		Different states have different tax costs and you will want to verify this figure with your Title Company, courthouse, or loan officer

1300   ADDITIONAL SETTLEMENT CHARGES:

Any additional charges incurred during the loan processes that have not been addressed previously will be explained and entered within the final area of the good faith estimate.

1301	Survey	Many lenders accept a survey affidavit from the Title Company as verification of the property location and boundary lines.
		If a survey must be performed for the property to clear underwriting, these charges are negotiated as paid by you or seller on the sales agreement.
1302	Pest Inspections	Pest Inspections are required by some loan programs and you have the right to request that a pest inspection be completed on the property as a condition of the purchase.
		The payment for these fees is negotiated on the Real Estate Sales Agreement.
		These payments are paid to the inspection provider based on a billing presented at the closing table.
1303	Flood Certification	A Flood Certification or verification that the property is not in a flood plain may be requested by underwriting or you can order one yourself if you have incorporated acceptable flood status as a condition of the purchase.
		If the flood certification is completed through a service retained by underwriting, the costs of the certification are paid to the lender at the time of closing and the lender

pays the certification service.

If another certification service is used to verify the flood status of the property, the name of the service will be entered into the good faith estimate and the charges imposed by the service included.

Payment to the service provider may be made during the loan process or as part of the settlement process. You will usually be responsible for these costs but you can negotiate with the seller about payment.

| 1304 | Courier Fees | Courier Fees may be charged by either the funding company or closing company for the transfer of documents via courier. |

Lender:			Sales Price:	
Address:			Base Loan Amount:	
			Total Loan Amount:	
Applicant(s):			Interest Rate:	
			Type of Loan:	
Property Address:			Preparation Date:	
			Loan Number	

The information provided below reflects estimates of the charges, which you are likely to incur at the settlement of your loan. The fees listed are estimates – actual charges may be more or less. Your transaction may not involve a fee for every item listed. THE NUMBERS LISTED BESIDE THE ESTIMATES GENERALLY CORRESPOND TO THE NUMBERED LINES CONTAINED THE HUD-1 OR HUD-1A SETTLEMENT STATEMENT WHICH YOU WILL BE RECEIVEING AT THE SETTLEMENT. THE HUD-1 OR HUD-1A SETTLEMENT STATEMENT WILL SHOW YOU THE ACTUAL COST FOR ITEMS PAID AT SETTLEMENT.

800	ITEMS PAYABLE IN CONNECTION WITH LOAN;		1100	TITLE CHARGES	
801	Origination Fee @ % + $	$2550.00	1101	Closing or Escrow Fee	$ 295.00
802	Discount Fee @ %+$	$	1102	Abstract or Title Search	$
803	Appraisal Fee	$ 275.00	1103	Title Examination	$
804	Credit Report	$ 50.00	1105	Document Preparation Fee	$
805	Lender's Inspection Fee	$	1106	Notary Fee	$ 35.00
806	Mortgage Insurance Fee	$	1107	Attorney's Fee	$
807	Assumption Fee	$	1108	Title Insurance	$ 618.75
808	Mortgage Broker Fee	$			$
810	Tax Related Service Fee	$ 98.00			$
811	Application Fee	$			$
812	Commitment Fee	$			$
813	Lender's Rate Lock-In Fee	$ 200.00			$
814	Processing Fee	$ 250.00			$
815	Underwriting Fee	$ 400.00			$
816	Wire Transfer Fee	$			$

900	ITEMS TO BE PAI DIN ADVANCE ;		1200	GOVERNMENT RECORDING AND TRANSFER	
901	Interest for 1 days @ $13.78 day	$ 13.78	1201	Recording Fee	$ 33.50
902	Mortgage Insurance Premium	$	1202	City/County Tax/Stamps	$ 80.00
903	Hazard Insurance Premium	$ 420.00	1203	State Tax/Stamps	$ 80.00
904	County Property Taxes	$1320.00	1205	Intangible Tax	$
905	Flood Insurance	$			$
		$			$

1000	RESERVES DEPOSITED WITH LENDER		1300	ADDITIONAL SETTLEMENT CHARGES	
1001	Hazard Ins 3 Mo @ $ 35 Per Mo	$ 105.00	1201	Survey	$
1002	Mortgage Ins. Mo@$ Per Mo	$	1202	Pest Inspection	$
1004	Tax & Assmt. 7 Mo@$110 Per Mo	$ 770.00	1203		$
1006	Flood Insurance	$	1205		$
				TOTAL ESTIMATED SETTLMENT CHARGES $	

S/B designates these costs to be paid by Seller / Broker   A designates those costs effecting APR

TOTAL ESTIMATED MONTHLY PAYMENT		TOTAL ESTIMATED FUNDS TO CLOSE	
Principal & Interest	$ 616.00	Real Estate Taxes	$ 110.00
Down Payment	$	Hazard Insurance	$ 35.00
Estimated Closing Costs	$7743.03	Flood Insurance	$
Estimated Prepaid Items	$	Mortgage Insurance	$
Total Paid Items (subtract)	$	Other	$
Other	$		
TOTAL MONTHLY PAYMENT	$ 761.00	CASH FROM BORROWER	$

APPROVED SERVICE PROVIDER LIST

Some mortgage lenders will use specific service providers when completing the processing and closing of your loan application. If the mortgage lender uses a specific service provider and you will be responsible for the billing that is incurred because of this use, the lender must provide a disclosure to you detailing this use so that you have the opportunity to make an informed decision applicable to the costs that they will incur.

APPROVED SERVICE PROVIDER LIST

Addendum to the standard "Good Faith Estimate" of Settlement Costs

_____ requires the use of certain providers in the processing and settlement of your loan. These providers are chosen from an approved list and we require that you pay for all portions of the services provided from these providers. The costs of these services are based on the charges of these providers or industry standards. Please refer to your attached Good Faith Estimate form for an estimate of each proposed charge. The following providers have been repeatedly used for the designated services within the last 12 months.

1.   CREDIT REPORTING AGENCIES:

2.   APPRAISAL SERVICES:

3.   PRIVATE MORTGAGE INSURANCE PROVIDERS:

4.   OTHER:

I/we acknowledge that we received a copy of this notice:

_____   _____
Borrower Signature   Date

_____   _____
Co-Borrower Signature   Date

6:6 Sample Form– Approved Service Provider List – HUD Release

Chapter 7

THE LOAN APPLICATION

The proper completion of the loan application, or 1003, will provide the details and information necessary to move your loan to closing. The lender's underwriting team will scrutinize each entry on the loan application and issue a loan approval based on these inclusions.

The documentation that you provide over the course of the loan process will support the entries on your loan application.

The completion of the loan application and remittal of the necessary file documentation that will support these entries is critical to the structure, process, and closing of the loan.

Your loan officer will assist you in completing the loan application. It is important that you review every entry on the finished application before signing the document. The entire loan will be structured around the information contained within the application and the supporting document that you submit. If there is an error on the application, your entire mortgage process could be delayed.

Uniform Residential Loan Application

This application is designed to be completed by the applicant(s) with the Lender's assistance. Applicants should complete this form as "Borrower" or "Co-Borrower", as applicable. Co-Borrower information must also be provided (and the appropriate box checked) when ___ the income or assets of a person other than the "Borrower" (Including Borrower's spouse) will be used as a basis for loan qualification or ___ the income or assets of the Borrower's spouse will not be used as a basis for loan qualification, but his or her liabilities must be considered because the Borrower resides in a community property state, the security property is located in a community property state or the borrower is relying on other property located in a community property state for repayment of the loan.

I. TYPE OF MORTGAGE AND TERMS OF LOAN

Mortgage Applied for:	__ VA __ Conventional __ Other __ FHA __ FmHA	Agency Case Number	Lender Case Number
Amount $	Interest Rate %	No of Months	Amortization Type __ Fixed Rate __ GPM	__ Other (explain) __ ARM (type)

II. PROPERTY INFORMATION AND PURPOSE OF LOAN

Subject Property Address (street, city, state, & zip code)		No Of Units
Legal Description of Subject Property (attach description if necessary)		Year Built

Purpose of Loan __ Purchase __ Construction __ Other (explain) __ Refinance __ Construction-Permanent	Property will be: __ Primary Residence __ Secondary Residence __ Investment

Complete this line if construction or construction-permanent loan

Year Lot Acquired	Original Cost $	Amount Existing Liens $	(a) Present Value of Lot	(b) Cost of Improvements	Total (a-b)

Complete this line if this is a refinance loan

Year Acquired	Original Cost $	Amount Existing Liens $	Purpose of Refinance	Describe Improvements __ made __ to be made Cost $

Title will be held in what Name(s)	Manner in which Title will be held	Estate will be held in __ Fee Simple
Source of Down Payment, Settlement Charges, and / or Subordinate Financing (explain)		__ Leasehold (show expiration date)

III BORROWER INFORMATION

Borrower	Co-Borrower
Borrowers Name (include Jr or Sr if applicable)	Co-Borrowers Name (include Jr or Sr if applicable)

Social Security Number	Home Phone	Age	Yrs School	Social Security Number	Home Phone	Age	Yrs School

__ Married __ Unmarried (include single __ Separated divorced, widowed)	Dependents (not listed by co-borrower) No / Ages	__ Married __ Unmarried (include single __ Separated divorced, widowed)	Dependents (not listed by borrower) No / Ages

Present Address (street, city, state, zip code) __ Own __ Rent No Yrs	Present Address (street, city, state, zip code) __ Own __ Rent No Yrs

If residing at present address less than two years, complete the following

Former Address (street, city, state, zip code) __ Own __ Rent No Yrs	Former Address (street, city, state, zip code) __ Own __ Rent No Yrs
Former Address (street, city, state, zip code) __ Own __ Rent No Yrs	Former Address (street, city, state, zip code) __ Own __ Rent No Yrs

IV EMPLOYMENT INFORMATION

Borrower	Co-Borrower
Name & Address of Employer __ Self Employed	Years on this Job Years employed in this line of work or profession	Name & Address of Employer __ Self Employed	Years on this Job Years employed in this line of work or profession
Position/Title/Type of Business	Business Phone	Position/Title/Type of Business	Business Phone

If employed in current position less than two years or if currently employed in more than position, complete the following:

Name & Address of Employer __ Self Employed	Dates (from-to) Monthly Income $	Name & Address of Employer __ Self Employed	Dates (from-to) Monthly Income $
Position/Title/Type of Business	Business Phone	Position/Title/Type of Business	Business Phone
Name & Address of Employer __ Self Employed	Dates (from-to) Monthly Income $	Name & Address of Employer __ Self Employed	Dates (from-to) Monthly Income $
Position/Title/Type of Business	Business Phone	Position/Title/Type of Business	Business Phone

7:1 Sample Form– 1003 Uniform Residential Loan Application – HUD Release

136

I. TYPE OF MORTGAGE AND TERMS OF LOAN				
Mortgage __ VA __ Conventional __ Other Applied for: __ FHA __ FmHA			Agency Case Number	Lender Case Number
Amount $	Interest Rate %	No of Months	Amortization __ Fixed Rate __ Other (explain) Type __ GPM ___ ARM (type)	

7:2 Sample Form– Extraction 1003 Uniform Residential Loan Application – HUD Release

The upper portion of the 1003, *Type of Mortgage and Terms of Loan,* contains file copy data and details relating to type of loan that you have chosen.

Type of Mortgage
The loan officer will check the box for the loan type that they have chosen for you.

This ensures that the proper guidelines are applied to the prequalification and approval processes.

Agency Case Number
The agency case number is the file tracking number assigned by the individuals who underwrite, pre-qualify, and approve the loan package.

Lender Case Number
The lender case number is the internal case number that your loan officer assigns to the file.

Terms of Loan
The terms of loan section of the 1003 refers to the type of mortgage that you are requesting.

These numbers are based on the calculation that your loan officer performs using the product matrix charts and an assessment of your needs.

When you submit an application for a pre-approval without a property in mind, the loan officer will enter the highest loan amount that you feel comfortable with given your specific situation and needs. This will be the pre-approval number and may be subject to a change when you have chosen a home to purchase.

Interest Rate

The information you enter relating to interest rate is also preliminary unless you have locked the offered interest rate.

Number of Months

The number of months refers to the amortization term of the loan that you have agreed to for your loan.

Amortization Type

The amortization type is the method that will be applied to the loan.

II. PROPERTY INFORMATION AND PURPOSE OF LOAN						
Subject Property Address (street, city, state, & zip code)						No Of Units
Legal Description of Subject Property (attach description if necessary)						Year Built
Purpose of Loan __ Purchase __ Construction __ Other (explain) __ Refinance __ Construction-Permanent				Property will be: __Primary __ Secondary __ Investment Residence Residence		
Complete this line if construction or construction-permanent loan						
Year Lot Acquired	Original Cost $	Amount Existing Liens $	(a) Present Value of Lot	(b) Cost of Improvements		Total (a-b)
Complete this line if this is a refinance loan						
Year Acquired	Original Cost $	Amount Existing Liens $	Purpose of Refinance	Describe Improvements __ made __ to be made Cost $		
Title will be held in what Name(s)			Manner in which Title will be held		Estate will be held in __ Fee Simple __ Leasehold (show expiration date)	
Source of Down Payment, Settlement Charges, and / or Subordinate Financing (explain)						

7:3 Sample Form– Extraction 1003 Uniform Residential Loan Application – HUD Release

Section 3 of the 1003 provides details relating to the *property* that is to be financed and the *purpose of the loan*.

Subject Property

If you have a sales agreement or know the address of the subject property, it will be entered into the loan application.

If you are requesting a pre-approval, with no property in mind, you or the loan officer will write, "to be decided" on the property address section.

All of the other information concerning the property will be determined once you have chosen a property and the application moves from a pre-approval to an actual loan package.

Number of Units
Federal Housing Acts and Loan Matrix treat properties differently based on the number of units in the property.

Example: You will enter a single-family property as 1.

Example: You will enter a duplex as 2.

Legal Description
The loan package documents will use the legal description of the property.

You can obtain the legal description from the sales agreement, public records system, previous title work, or other documentation provided to you by the real estate agent.

If the legal description information is too long to fit within the space provided, you or the loan officer will enter "*See Attached Legal Description*" and then attach an addendum page to the application that includes the full legal description of the property.

Year Built
The age of a property will affect various factors ranging from approval status to property valuation. You can obtain information about the age of the property from the Real Estate Agent, the Appraiser, or other sources.

Purpose of Loan
You will include information about the purpose of the loan.

A purchase, refinance, construction, construction to perm, and other types of loans will be handled differently during the loan processing stage. If you are unsure about the answer to this question, you should give the loan officer the purpose information so that they can help you complete this section.

Property Use/Occupancy

You must include information relating to how you intend to use the property.

- Primary residence

- A vacation home

- Secondary residence

- Investment property

The loan and loan terms you are offered will be different depending on how you intend to use the property. Owner occupied properties typically obtain a higher LTV status and lower interest rates.

Construction and Construction to Permanent

A loan for new construction requires different processing, approvals, and closing activities.

If the loan is a construction loan, you will incorporate information within the segment that relates to the construction status and costs.

This includes

- The year that you obtained the building lot

- The original cost of the lot

- Any existing liens on the property

- The current value of the lot

The details of the building lot added to the costs of the improvements planned using the loan funds enables underwriting to calculate a total property cost and value.

Refinance

If you are completing a refinance transaction, additional information that pertains to your history with the property will be needed.

If the loan is a refinance transaction, you must enter

- The year the property was acquired
- The original cost of the property
- Current liens against the property
- The purpose of the refinance:
    Cash Out
    Debt Consolidation
    Interest Rate Reduction
    Other

- You should provide a brief description of any improvements relating to the property.

Improvements are typically current improvements that are being made or improvements that will be made using the loan funds.

Many times when individuals apply for a property refinance, they will use some of the funds received during the refinance to complete improvement, renovations, or upgrades to the property. These actions will typically improve the property condition or value. If you are obtaining a refinance loan and plan to make improvements to the property using the loan proceeds, you should describe your plans within the loan submittal package.

Title
You should include information relating to the title of the property.

The manner that title will be held and the names of the individuals on the property will affect the security of the loan and may alter the individuals who must be included on the loan application.

Most loan guidelines require that any individual who will hold title as an owner of the property also be included on the mortgage loan application.

Source of Funds
The final entry in this section of the application pertains to the source of

the down payment, settlement charges, or other financial matters relating to loan.

You should enter source of the funds that you plan to use to complete the home purchase process.

Common examples of funds to close include

- Seller concessions toward closing costs

- Savings

- 401(k) withdrawals

- A gift from a friend or family member

It is a part of the loan officer's job to help you determine the best source of funds to use for their transaction.

Borrower				III BORROWER INFORMATION			Co-Borrower	
Borrowers Name (include Jr or Sr if applicable)					Co-Borrowers Name (include Jr or Sr if applicable)			
Social Security Number	Home Phone	Age	Yrs School		Social Security Number	Home Phone	Age	Yrs School
__ Married __ Unmarried (include single __ Separated divorced, widowed)		Dependents (not listed by co- borrower)			__ Married __ Unmarried (include single __ Separated divorced, widowed)		Dependents (not listed by borrower)	
		No	Ages				No	Ages
Present Address (street, city, state, zip code) __ Own __ Rent No Yrs					Present Address (street, city, state, zip code) __ Own __ Rent No Yrs			
If residing at present address less than two years, complete the following								
Former Address (street, city, state, zip code) __ Own __ Rent No Yrs					Former Address (street, city, state, zip code) __ Own __ Rent No Yrs			
Former Address (street, city, state, zip code) __ Own __ Rent No Yrs					Former Address (street, city, state, zip code) __ Own __ Rent No Yrs			

7:4 Sample Form– Extraction 1003 Uniform Residential Loan Application – HUD Release

You should provide accurate and complete personal information on the loan application. The information that you enter will be used to finalize your loan terms and to complete the loan closing documents.

Residence history
You should include a residence history that extends back 2 years. If additional space is necessary, they may include the information on the final page of the application.

Employment History
You will enter their employment information into the 1003.

The loan officer will verify and document this information through pay stubs, W-2's, and other documentation that you provide during the application meeting.

Employment information must extend back 2-years.

You may use the final page of the application to enter any employment details that do not fit within the designated space.

Additional Income
If you have income that does not relate to direct employment such as disability, child support, or other income, and you wish to use this income for qualifying purposes; you should enter it within the employment history field.

If you do not wish to use additional or other income for qualifying purposes but still wish to disclose it on the application as a compensating factor, you should enter the applicable details within the field labeled *"income not to be used for qualifying proposes"*.

You are not required to disclose this income if you do not wish to do so.

Continuation Period
Certain types of income will require a continuation period in order to be considered as qualifying income. This type of income requires that you prove that the income will continue into the future.

Example: Child support income requires documentation proving that the child support payments will continue for two years into the future in order for it to qualify as income used for loan qualification.

Each loan program will have a specified continuation period that they require and your loan officer can help you determine what is necessary to use income that requires continuation periods.

Uniform Residential Loan Application

V. MOTHLY INCOME AND COMBINED EXPENSE INFORMATION

Gross Monthly Income	Borrower	Co-Borrower	Total	Combined Monthly Housing Expenses	Present	Proposed
Self Empl Income *	$	$	$	Rent	$	
Overtime				First Mortgage (P&I)		$
Bonuses				Other Financing (P&I)		
Commissions				Hazard Insurance		
Dividends/Interest				Real Estate Taxes		
Net Rental Income				Mortgage Insurance		
Other (before completing see the notice in describe other income below)				Homeowner Assn Dues		
				Other		
Total	$	$	$	Total	$	$

* Self Employed Borrower(s) maybe be required to provide additional documentation such as tax returns and financial statements.

B/C	Describe Other Income Notice Alimony, child support or separate maintenance income need not be revealed if the Borrower (B) or Co-Borrower (C) doesn't choose to have it considered for repaying this loan.	Monthly Amount
		$
		$
		$

VI. ASSETS AND LIABILITIES

This Statement and any applicable supporting schedule may be completed jointly by both married and unmarried Co-Borrowers if their assets and liabilities are sufficiently joined so that the Statement can be meaningfully and fairly presented on a combined basis; otherwise separate Statements and Schedules are required. If the Co-Borrower section was completed about a spouse, this Statement; and supporting schedules must be completed about that spouse also.

ASSETS Description	Cash or Market Value	Liabilities and Pledged Assets List the creditors name, address and account numbers for outstanding debts including automobile loans, revolving charge accounts, real estate loans, alimony, child support, stock pledges, etc. Use continuation sheet if necessary. Indicate by (*) those liabilities which will be satisfied upon sale of real estate owned or upon refinancing of the subject property.		
Cash deposit toward purchase held by	$	LIABILITIES	Monthly Pmt & Mos Left To Pay	Unpaid Balance
List checking and savings accounts below Name and address of Bank, S&L, or Credit Union		Name and Address of Company	$ Payt / Mos	$
Acct no.	$	Acct No		
Name and address of Bank, S&L, or Credit Union		Name and Address of Company	$ Payt / Mos	$
Acct no.		Acct No		
Name and address of Bank, S&L, or Credit Union		Name and Address of Company	$ Payt / Mos	$
Acct no.	$	Acct No		
Name and address of Bank, S&L, or Credit Union		Name and Address of Company	$ Payt / Mos	$
Acct no.	$	Acct No		
Stocks & Bonds (company name/number & description)	$	Name and Address of Company	$ Payt / Mos	$
Life insurance net cash value Face amount: $	$			
Subtotal Liquid Assets	$	Acct No		
Real estate owned (enter market value) from schedule of real estate owned)	$	Name and Address of Company	$ Payt / Mos	$
Vested interest in retirement fund	$	Acct No		
Net worth of business(es) owned (attach financial statement)	$	Name and Address of Company Acct No	$ Payt / Mos	$
Automobiles owned (make and year)	$	Alimony/Child Support / Separate Maintenance Pmst)	$	
Other Assets	$	Job Related Expense (child care, union dues, etc.)	$	
		Total Monthly Payments	Total Liabilities b	
Total Assets	$	Net Worth (a minus b) $		$

7:5 Sample Form–1003 Uniform Residential Loan Application – HUD Release

144

Gross Monthly Income	Borrower	Co-Borrower	Total	Combined Monthly Housing Expenses	Present	Proposed
Self Empl Income *	$	$	$	Rent	$	
Overtime				First Mortgage (P&I)		$
Bonuses				Other Financing (P&I)		
Commissions				Hazard Insurance		
Dividends/Interest				Real Estate Taxes		
Net Rental Income				Mortgage Insurance		
Other (before completing see the notice in describe other income below)				Homeowner Assn Dues		
				Other		
Total	$	$	$	Total	$	$

7:6 Sample Form– Extraction 1003 Uniform Residential Loan Application – HUD Release

Page 3 of the 1003 will deal with *income, housing expense and credit related* matters.

Income and Expense

Your basic income overtime income, bonus income, commission income, or other income should mirror the income related to the job information that you included on page one of the application.

B/C	Describe Other Income Notice Alimony, child support or separate maintenance income need not be revealed if the Borrower (B) or Co-Borrower (C) doesn't choose to have it considered for repaying this loan.	Monthly Amount
		$
		$
		$

7:7 Sample Form– Extraction 1003 Uniform Residential Loan Application – HUD Release

Additional Income

At times, there may be income that cannot be used as qualifying income. This income will not be entered into the regular income and employment section.

Example: Child support payments that will only continue for 1 ½ years

This income cannot be considered as part of the base DTI income but by including it within the 1003; you strengthen the loan file and set the stage if your loan officer must request an exception later in the loan process.

In addition to income and assets, page 3 of the 1003 will address *present rent or mortgage payments* and the *proposed mortgage payment* that will exist after the loan is completed.

Combined Monthly Housing Expenses	Present	Proposed
Rent	$	
First Mortgage (P&I)		$
Other Financing (P&I)		
Hazard Insurance		
Real Estate Taxes		
Mortgage Insurance		
Homeowner Assn Dues		
Other		
Total	$	$

7:8 Sample Form– Extraction 1003 Uniform Residential Loan Application – HUD Release

Your loan officer will assist you in completing the financial data relating to your post-loan position.

You will enter the

- monthly housing expense
- any housing insurance payments
- the amount of real estate taxes you pay for your present home
- any mortgage insurance premium
- homeowner's association dues
- any other fixed housing expenses related to the property that you currently use as your primary residence

The total of all of these figures will be the current housing expense information.

You will enter the proposed mortgage payment for your new loan based on the

- loan amount
- amortization term
- interest rate

you have been offered.

You will also calculate

- insurance
- real estate taxes
- other expenses related to the home

You will total these, and this figure will act as the baseline for the housing expense ratio.

ASSETS Description	Cash or Market Value
Cash deposit toward purchase held by	$
List checking and savings accounts below	
Name and address of Bank, S&L, or Credit Union	
Acct no.	$
Name and address of Bank, S&L, or Credit Union	
Acct no.	
Name and address of Bank, S&L, or Credit Union	
Acct no.	$
Name and address of Bank, S&L, or Credit Union	
Acct no.	$
Stocks & Bonds (company name/number & description)	$
Life insurance net cash value Face amount: $	$
Subtotal Liquid Assets	$
Real estate owned (enter market value) from schedule of real estate owned)	$
Vested interest in retirement fund	$
Net worth of business(es) owned (attach financial statement)	$
Automobiles owned (make and year)	$
Other Assets	$
Total Assets	$

Assets

In addition to income, assets will be considered as part of the approval process.

The information that you enter here will be used to verify the availability of the funds that you have indicated will be used as the source of funds to close.

Example: Bank accounts and other savings will typically require the use of the VOD form.

VOD forms are included within the documentation section of the coursework.

You should review the use and completion of these forms as well as the other documentation requirements to ensure that you have an understanding of how loan funds and assets will be verified.

7:9 Sample Form– Extraction 1003 Uniform Residential Loan Application – HUD Release

Liabilities and Pledged Assets List the creditor's name, address and account numbers for outstanding debts including automobile loans, revolving charge accounts, real estate loans, alimony, child support, stock pledges, etc. Use continuation sheet if necessary. Indicate by (*) those liabilities which will be satisfied upon sale of real estate owned or upon refinancing of the subject property.

LIABILITIES	Monthly Pmt & Mos Left To Pay	Unpaid Balance
Name and Address of Company	$ Payt / Mos	$
Acct No		
Name and Address of Company	$ Payt / Mos	$
Acct No		
Name and Address of Company	$ Payt / Mos	$
Acct No		
Name and Address of Company	$ Payt / Mos	$
Acct No		
Name and Address of Company	$ Payt / Mos	$
Acct No		
Name and Address of Company	$ Payt / Mos	$
Acct No		
Name and Address of Company	$ Payt / Mos	
Acct No		
Alimony/Child Support / Separate Maintenance Pmt)	$	
Job Related Expense (childcare, union dues, etc.)	$	
Total Monthly Payments	Total Liabilities b	
Net Worth (a minus b) $		

7:10 Sample Form– Extraction 1003 Uniform Residential Loan Application – HUD Release

Liabilities

The segment relating to recurring debts will often be exported directly from the credit report. You may be required to enter the data regarding debts from the credit report by hand if your loan officer is not able to auto-fill these fields.

You will want to verify that all of the debt exported to the liability section of the 1003 is accurate.

If you are aware of any debt that is not included on the credit report, you must enter the information by hand.

Example: If you pay child support o another individual, you should attach documentation showing how much the payments are on a monthly basis and how long the payments will continue.

This information must be entered into the 1003 liability section.

VI ASSETS AND LIABILITIES (cont)							
Schedule of Real Estate Owned (if additional properties are owned use continuation sheet)							
Property Address (enter S if sold, PS if pending sale or r if a rental being held for income)		Type of Property	Present Market Value	Amount of Mortgage/Liens	Gross Rental Income	Mortgage Payments	Insurance Maintenance & Taxes	Net Rental Income
			$	$	$	$	$	$
	Total		$	$	$	$	$	$

7:11 Sample Form– Extraction 1003 Uniform Residential Loan Application – HUD Release

Real Estate

Any additional real estate that you own but is not selling during this transaction should be defined within the application.

The assets and history from this real estate may be considered a compensating factor.

List any additional names under which credit has previously been received and indicate appropriate creditor name(s) and account number(s)		
Alternative Name	Creditor Name	Account Number

7:12 Sample Form– Extraction 1003 Uniform Residential Loan Application – HUD Release

Aliases

You may have used a different name or a variation of you full name when applying for past credit.

Example: A married woman will often establish credit under her maiden name. The name change upon marriage could confuse the credit history report unless you report the maiden name.

VII DETAILS OF TRANSACTION		
a. Purchase Price	$	
b. Alterations, improvements, repairs		
c. Land (if acquired separately)		
d. Refinance (include items to be paid off)		
e. Estimated prepaid items		
g. PMI, MIP, Funding Fee paid in cash		
h. Discount (if Borrower will pay)		
i. Total costs (add a through h)		
j. Subordinate Financing		
k. Borrower's closing costs paid by seller	(	)
l. Other credits (explain)		
m. Loan amount (exclude PMI, MIP, Funding Fee financed)		
n. PMI, MIP, Funding Fee financed		
o. Loan Amount (add m & n)		
p. Cash from/to Borrower (j, k, l & o from i)		

7:13 Sample Form– Extraction 1003 Uniform Residential Loan Application – HUD Release

The *details of transaction* section of the 1003 will summarize all of the mathematical and structural planning that your loan officer has completed as part of the application process.

The details of the transaction numbers will automatically export as part of the application process in applications that are computer generated. Hand calculated applications require that your loan officer enter these figures manually

Regardless of the method of entry, you should review the details of the transaction carefully to ensure that all entries match the details of the loan as you understand them.

- The loan officer will enter the purchase price of the property or the refinance amount being requested into the 1003.

  If there is no property attached to the loan, and the package is being submitted for a pre-approval, the loan officer will want to ask for the highest loan amount you are eligible to receive based on ratios.

The loan amount request can be lowered later in the process, however, a higher loan request will require that the underwriting department recalculate all numbers and issue an entirely new approval. New approval documents and disclosures will be issued on a lowered loan amount, but the approval will not need to be re-underwritten to determine if you can afford a higher loan amount.

- Once you have obtained a sales agreement, the loan officer will want to verify other details beyond just the purchase price.

  The sales agreement can include any item negotiated between you and the seller.

  A commonly negotiated matter is seller concession toward your closing costs. The loan officer will need to ensure that any negotiated financial matter incorporated into the sales agreement is entered into the financial details section of the 1003.

- Some loan programs will require that you pay certain items in advance.

  Any item that will be pre-paid before the date of closing should be entered into the details of transaction.

+ The loan officer will enter the closing costs figures directly from the good faith estimate that you are given.

  The good faith estimate may need to be revised at the time that you choose a property.

+ If the loan program applicable to the transaction requires that you obtain PMI, any cash premium associated with the insurance should be entered into the details of the transaction.

+ At times, you may choose to pay discount points as part of the transaction.

  If the funds are available to pay discount points and you choose to use this option, the loan officer will need to ensure that the quoted interest rate evident on the 1003 and applicable monthly payment reflects these discount points.

The loan officer should enter the total amount paid toward discount into the details of the transaction.

=   All costs related to the loan will be totaled.

-    Subordinate financing or second loans will be added into the details of the transaction.

+   Any closing costs that the seller has agreed to pay on your behalf must be documented on the sales agreement and entered as a credit on the details of the transaction.

+   If there are additional credits allocated to you as a part of the process, the loan officer should include the amounts within the details of the transaction summary.

-    The loan amount that you will receive because of the transaction should be entered. This loan amount entry should not include any PMI premium that is financed as part of the agreed upon loan terms. Financed PMI premiums will be entered separately under the designated field.

=   All of the figures will then be totaled and a final figure for cash from OR to you will be included within the details of the transaction. Cash to you typically results from a refinancing transaction but may result if you receive a higher loan amount or pay higher up-front payments.

•   Cash from you will usually be an included figure in a purchase transaction.

The cash from the borrower entry is the amount of funds that you must bring to the closing table. Using these funds will usually require proof that these funds exist and are your own money.

You should receive a copy of the 1003. If there is any information on the 1003 that is incorrect or that you do not understand, you must bring it to the attention of your loan officer.

CREDIT REPORT AUTHORIZATION AND RELEASE

Authorization is hereby granted to _____ to obtain a standard factual data credit report through a credit-reporting agency chosen by
_____
___.

My signature below authorizes the release to the credit-reporting agency a copy of my credit application, and authorizes the credit-reporting agency to obtain information regarding my employment, savings accounts, and outstanding credit accounts (mortgages, auto loans, personal loans, charge cards, credit unions, etc.) Authorization is further granted to the reporting agency to use a Photostatted reproduction of this authorization if necessary to obtain any information regarding the above-mentioned information.

Applicants hereby request a copy of the credit report with any possible derogatory information be sent to the address of present residence, and holds
_____ and any credit reporting organization harmless in so mailing the copy requested.

Any reproduction of this credit authorization and release made by reliable means (for example, photocopy, or facsimile is considered an original.

7:14 Sample Form– Credit Report Authorization and Release – HUD Release

CREDIT DENIAL LETTER

Dear Applicant:

Thank you for your recent mortgage application. Your request for a loan was carefully considered, and we regret that we are unable to approve your application at this time.

This decision is based on the following factor(s):

__ Insufficient income to meet our minimum requirement
__ Insufficient income to sustain payments on the amount of credit requested
__ Income could not be verified
__ Employment history is not of sufficient length to qualify
__ Employment history could not be verified
__ Credit history of timely payments is unsatisfactory
__ Credit history could not be verified
__ Lack of sufficient credit references
__ Lack of acceptable types of credit references
__ Current obligations are excessive in relationship to income
__ Other _____

We will keep your application on file and look forward to working with you in the near future when your situation has changed.

The consumer-reporting agency that provided information that influenced our decision in whole or in part was (*Name, Address, and Telephone Number of Reporting Agency*). The reporting agency is unable to provide specific reasons why we have denied credit to you. You have the right to know the information contained in your credit file under the Fair Credit Reporting Act. Any questions regarding such information should be directed to (Credit Reporting Agency).

7:15 Sample Form– Credit Denial Letter – HUD Release

CHAPTER 8

APPRAISALS

A comprehensive understanding of appraisals is another area in which you must obtain knowledge. Much of the loan process focuses on you. An important factor that everyone involved in the transaction must consider is that the property is as important as you are in the loan process.

It is critical that the property condition and value matches the amount you are spending to obtain the property.

The lender will scrutinize property appraisals and other property related information to ensure that the money that they lend you is secure in the event you default. You should scrutinize the property appraisal and property related information to ensure that the property condition is as you expect.

Sometimes an appraisal will contain what is termed a red flag. A red flag is any information that indicates an issue exists that will lower the value of the property.

Appraisers are important elements in a variety of components of the lending process. The valuation and accuracy of an appraisal must be dependable. Appraisals will be used for

- Sales Price Negotiation
- Loan-to-Value Assessment
- Collateral Security

- Homeowner's Insurance Policies

- Title Insurance Policies

- Equity

- Determining necessary repairs to the property

- Private Mortgage Insurance Premiums

This is not to be considered an all-inclusive list. The listing is a basic assessment of the appraisal uses. Appraisals may affect other facets of the mortgage and home-buying process.

Many lenders have approved appraisers that they prefer to have complete the appraisal on any property being considered for a loan. The approval of an appraiser is based on the historical ability of that appraiser to provide appraisals that reflect the fair value of the property and do not contain exceptions to the preferred appraisal guidelines of the lender.

You will select an appraiser for your property from the list provided to you by the loan officer. At times, you will pay the appraisal fee up-front. This pre-payment helps to ensure that the appraiser is paid in the event that you do not finish the home purchase process. If you do not pre-pay the appraiser, the cost of the appraisal will be included as part of the settlement charges.

Most appraisals are completed using a form called the *Uniform Residential Appraisal Report* or URAR.

UNIFORM RESIDENTIAL APPRAISAL REPORT

The purpose of this summary appraisal report is to provide with an accurate, and adequately supported opinion of market value of the subject property

Property Address	City	State	Zip Code

Borrower	Owner of Public Record	County

Legal Description

Assessor's Parcel #	Tax Year	R.E. Taxes $	

Neighborhood Name	Map Reference	Census Tract	

Occupant __ Owner __ Tenant __ Vacant   Special Assessments $ __ PUD HOA $ ____ per year __ per month

Property Rights Appraised ___ Fee Simple ___ Leasehold ___ Other (describe)

Assignment Type ___ Purchase Transaction ___ Refinance Transaction ___ Other (describe)

Lender Client   Address

Is the subject property currently offered for sale or has it been offered for sale in the twelve months prior to the effective date of this appraisal __ yes __ no

Report data source(s) used offering prices(s), and date(s)

I __ did __ did not analyze the contract for sale for the subject purchase transaction. Explain the results of the analysis of the contract for sale or why analysis was not performed.

Contract Price $ Date of Contract   Is the property seller the owner of public record __ Yes __ No Data Source(s)

Is there any financial assistance (loan charges, sale concessions, gift or down payment assistance, etc.) to be paid by any party on behalf of the borrower? __ Yes __ No If yes, report the total dollar amount and describe the items to be paid.

Note: Race and racial composition of the neighborhood are not appraisal factors

Neighborhood Characteristics			One-Unit Housing Trends				One-Unit Housing	Present Land Use %	
Location	Urban	Suburban Rural	Property Values	Increasing	Stable	Declining	PRICE AGE	One-Unit	%
Built-Up	Over 75%	25-75% Under 25%	Demand Supply	Shortage	In Balance	Over Supply	$ (000) (yrs)	2-4 Unit	%
Growth	Rapid	Stable Slow	Marketing Time	Under 2 mth	3-6 mths	Over 6 mths	Low	Multi-Family	%
Neighborhood Boundaries							High	Commercial	%
							Pred.	Other	%

Neighborhood Description

Market Conditions (including support for the above conclusions)

Dimension	Area	Shape	View

Specific Zoning Classification   Zoning Description

Zoning Compliance __ Legal __ Legal Nonconforming (Grandfathered use) __ No Zoning __ Illegal (describe)

Is the highest and best use of the subject property as improved (or as proposed per plans and specifications) the present use? __ Yes __ No If No, describe

Utilities   Public   Other (describe)   Public   Other (describe)   Off-site Improvements – Type   Public   Private

Electricity	Water	Street
Gas	Sanitary Sewer	Alley

FEMA Special Hazard Area __ Yes __ No FEMAL Flood Zone   Fema Map #   FEMA Map Date

Are the utilities and off-site improvements typical for the market area __ Yes __ No If No, describe

Are there any adverse site conditions or extreme factors (easements, encroachments, environmental conditions and uses, etc.)? __ Yes __ No If Yes, describe

General Description	Foundation		Exterior Description materials/condition	Interior materials/condition
Units One One w Accessory Unit	Concrete Slab	Crawl Space	Foundation Walls	Floors
# of Stories	Full Basement	Partial Basement	Exterior Walls	Walls
Type Det Att S-Dec / End Unit	Basement Area sq ft		Roof Surface	Trim/Finish
Existing Proposed Under Cons	Basement Finish %		Gutters & Downspouts	Bath Floor
Design (Style)	Outside Entry/ Exist Sump Pump		Window Type	Bath Wainscot
Year Built	Evidence of __ Infestation		Storm Sash / Insulated	Car Storage None
Effective Age (Yrs)	Dampness Settlement		Screens	Driveway # of Cars
Attic None	Heating FWA HWBB Radiant		Amenities Woodstove(s)	Driveway Surface
Drop Stair Stairs	Other Fuel		Fireplaces # Fence	Garage # of Cars
Floor Scuttle	Cooling Central Air Conditioning		Patio/Deck Porch	Carport # of Cars
Finished Heated	Individual Other		Pool Other	Att Det Built-in

Appliances   Refrigerator   Range/Oven   Dishwasher   Disposal   Microwave   Washer/Dryer   Other (describe)

Finished area above grade contains: Rooms   Bedrooms   Bath(s)   Square Feet of Gross Living Area Above Grade

Additional Features (special energy efficient items, etc.)

Describe the conditions of the property (including needed repairs, deterioration, renovations, remodeling, etc.)

Are there any physical deficiencies or adverse conditions that affect the livability, soundness, or structural integrity of the property? __ Yes __ No If Yes, describe

8:1 Sample Form– URAR – Uniform Residential Appraisal Report – HUD Release

Subject

Property Address		City	State	Zip Code
Borrower	Owner of Public Record		County	
Legal Description				
Assessor's Parcel #		Tax Year	R.E. Taxes $	
Neighborhood Name		Map Reference	Census Tract	
Occupant __ Owner __ Tenant __ Vacant	Special Assessments $	__ PUD HOA $	__ per year __ per month	
Property Rights Appraised __ Fee Simple __ Leasehold __ Other (describe)				
Assignment Type __ Purchase Transaction __ Refinance Transaction __ Other (describe)				

8:2 Sample Form Extraction - URAR – Uniform Residential Appraisal Report – HUD Release

The upper portion of the URAR contains identifying data, general details of the property being assessed, and information relating to the individuals involved in the transaction.

The appraiser may note any special assessments related to the property you are purchasing. You are responsible for paying any assessments related to the property after you complete your purchase. You should review this section to ensure that there are no surprise costs involved in your new property ownership. If these assessments are recurring costs, they will affect your DTI ratios. These assessments will become a factor in the borrower's DTI ratio.

The appraiser will define the rights being appraised. This section of the URAR refers to the rights that are available for transfer by the current owner of the property.

Property Rights Appraised

> Fee Simple
> Leasehold
> Other

The rights being transferred through the transaction may alter your ability to use your new property. You should review this section to make sure that you have an understanding of the rights that you are purchasing. Most transactions will be fee simple transactions giving you full rights to the property.

The appraiser will note the type of transaction being conducted.

Assignment Type

Purchase Transaction
Refinance Transaction
Other

You should review each entry within this section and confirm that these entries match your expectations.

If you note an error in a document, you should discuss the error with your loan officer. The loan officer will take steps to have the discrepancy corrected.

Contract

I __ did __ did not analyze the contract for sale for the subject purchase transaction. Explain the results of the analysis of the contract for sale or why analysis was not performed.
Contract Price $ Date of Contract Is the property seller the owner of public record __ Yes __ No Data Source(s)
Is there any financial assistance (loan charges, sale concessions, gift or down payment assistance, etc.) to be paid by any party on behalf of the borrower? __ Yes __ No If yes, report the total dollar amount and describe the items to be paid.

8:3 Sample Form Extraction - URAR – Uniform Residential Appraisal Report – HUD Release

Data pertaining to any sales contract or other contract that is a part of the transaction will be included within this section.

You, your loan officer, or the real estate agent will wish to supply a copy of the contract to the appraiser at the time of the appraisal request.

Upon receipt of the completed appraisal, you should review the inclusions within this section to confirm that they match the details of the transaction you negotiated with the seller.

Neighborhood

Note: Race and racial composition of the neighborhood are not appraisal factors									
Neighborhood Characteristics			One-Unit Housing Trends				One-Unit Housing	Present Land Use %	
Location	Urban	Suburban	Rural	Property Values	Increasing	Stable	Declining	PRICE AGE	One-Unit %
Built-Up	Over 75%	25-75%	Under 25%	Demand Supply	Shortage	In Balance	Over Supply	$ (000) (yrs)	2-4 Unit %
Growth	Rapid	Stable	Slow	Marketing Time	Under 2 mth	3-6 mths	Over 6 mths	Low	Multi-Family %
Neighborhood Boundaries								High	Commercial %
								Pred.	Other %
Neighborhood Description									

8:4 Sample Form Extraction - URAR – Uniform Residential Appraisal Report – HUD Release

Details concerning the neighborhood of the property will be considered during the appraisal process.

Each line of the neighborhood assessment should be completed by the appraiser. There should be no blank lines or unchecked boxes. You should review the neighborhood information to gain an understanding of the area where you will soon live.

Neighborhood Red Flags

Assessments within the neighborhood section present vital information that may affect the value of your property.

You should review the neighborhood data to ensure that the appraiser's opinion of your new neighborhood matches your expectations. If there is an entry that you do not understand or that does not match your expectations, you should discuss it with your loan officer.

Market Characteristics and Conditions

Market Conditions (including support for the above conclusions)

8:5 Sample Form Extraction - URAR – Uniform Residential Appraisal Report – HUD Release

The appraiser will provide an assessment of market comparison and market conditions. You should review the appraiser's comments. Any comment that could be considered a negative factor may affect your loan approval and the value of your property. If the appraiser states that the market for property similar to the subject property is below average, the security inherent in the property may be lessened. If your property is not what you expected, you may want to choose another home to purchase or renegotiate the purchase agreement with the seller.

Site

Dimension	Area	Shape	View
Specific Zoning Classification	Zoning Description		
Zoning Compliance Legal Legal Nonconforming (Grandfathered use) No Zoning Illegal (describe)			
Is the highest and best use of the subject property as improved (or as proposed per plans and specifications) the present use? Yes No If No, describe			
Utilities Public Other (describe)	Public Other (describe)	Off-site Improvements – Type Public Private	
Electricity	Water	Street	
Gas	Sanitary Sewer	Alley	
FEMA Special Hazard Area Yes No FEMAL Flood Zone	Fema Map #	FEMA Map Date	
Are the utilities and off-site improvements typical for the market area Yes No If No, describe			
Are there any adverse site conditions or extreme factors (easements, encroachments, environmental conditions and uses, etc.)? Yes No If Yes, describe			

8:6 Sample Form Extraction - URAR – Uniform Residential Appraisal Report – HUD Release

The site segment of the appraisal describes the parcel where your property is built and any issue regarding site usages that are apparent.

Any issues with the use of the land including easements, encroachment, boundary line issues, or other factors affecting the land will affect how you can use your new property and may affect the value of your new purchase. If any item entered on the appraisal is not what you expected, you may wish to choose another property or renegotiate with the seller regarding the correction of any site usage issues discovered during the process. The payment for this correction is a common point of post-sales agreement negotiation.

Improvements

General Description	Foundation	Exterior Description materials/condition	Interior materials/condition
Units One One w Accessory Unit	Concrete Slab Crawl Space	Foundation Walls	Floors
# of Stories	Full Basement Partial Basement	Exterior Walls	Walls
Type Det Att S-Dec / End Unit	Basement Area sq ft	Roof Surface	Trim/Finish
Existing Proposed Under Cons	Basement Finish %	Gutters & Downspouts	Bath Floor
Design (Style)	Outside Entry/ Exist Sump Pump	Window Type	Bath Wainscot
Year Built	Evidence of Infestation	Storm Sash / Insulated	Car Storage None
Effective Age (Yrs)	Dampness Settlement	Screens	Driveway # of Cars
Attic None	Heating FWA HWBB Radiant	Amenities Woodstove(s)	Driveway Surface
Drop Stair Stairs	Other Fuel	Fireplaces # Fence	Garage # of Cars
Floor Scuttle	Cooling Central Air Conditioning	Patio/Deck Porch	Carport # of Cars
Finished Heated	Individual Other	Pool Other	Att Det Built-in
Appliances Refrigerator Range/Oven	Dishwasher Disposal Microwave	Washer/Dryer Other (describe)	
Finished area above grade contains: Rooms	Bedrooms	Bath(s) Square Feet of Gross Living Area Above Grade	
Additional Features (special energy efficient items, etc.)			
Describe the conditions of the property (including needed repairs, deterioration, renovations, remodeling, etc.)			
Are there any physical deficiencies or adverse conditions that affect the livability, soundness, or structural integrity of the property? Yes No If Yes, describe			

8:7 Sample Form Extraction - URAR – Uniform Residential Appraisal Report – HUD Release

Many of the red flags that occur from the prospective of the lender will occur in the area of the appraisal that relates to the improvements. The term improvement refers to the actual building of the property. All portions of your new property should obtain at least a rating of average.

If any area relating to the property receives a rating of less than average, you may want to negotiate with the seller to determine the steps that will need to be taken to improve the rating or condition of the property and who will pay for these repairs or modifications.

The appraiser will check the boxes that relate to the property.

of Units
These will include the number of units contained within the property.

of Stories
The number of stories included in the property will affect the desirability of the property. The comparables used for the valuation portion of the appraisal should be of a similar number of stories.

Status
The appraiser will note the status of the property including whether the improvements are existing, under construction or planned improvements. The status of the property should match the loan type that you are requesting.

Example: Proposed Improvements =   Construction Loan

Design
The design of the property will affect the desirability of the property. The comparables used for the valuation portion of the appraisal should be of a similar design and appeal. You should check these areas to ensure that they match your expectations.

Year Built and Effective Age
The year that the property was built and the effective age of the property will affect the value. The year built is the actual age. Improvements, renovations, and updating are factored into the effective age. A home may be a number of decades old and have a much younger effective

age if the property has been renovated to bring it into line with newer construction.

Attic
The inclusion or exclusion of an attic may affect both the desirability and the value of a property. Square foot value is typically assessed to those areas that are heated and cooled. These areas are considered to be living square feet. If the attic is used as living square feet, it will be factored as part of the dollar per square foot valuation process. You should check this area to ensure that they match your expectations.

Foundation
The type of foundation, including the type of basement that they property contains will effect both the desirability and the value of the property. Similar to an attic, a finished basement with a heat source may be considered as living square footage and factored as part of the dollar per square foot valuation. You should check this area to ensure that they match your expectations.

Issues
The appraiser will note any issues that are apparent in the basement area of the property. Any issues, including dampness, infestation, or settlement of the property may need to be addressed before the loan can proceed to closing. These issues may put the value and condition of the property at risk if left unaddressed. You will wish to review any entries relating to issues found by the appraiser carefully. You may wish to cancel the purchase or negotiate the repair of these issues with the seller.

Heating / Cooling
The type of heating and cooling contained within the property may affect the value and appeal of the property. You should check these areas to ensure that they match your expectations.

Exterior/Interior
The interior and exterior of the property should be in good condition. You should check this area to ensure that they match your expectations. The condition rating set by the appraiser should be at least average. Any condition rating below average may need to be addressed before the loan can proceed to closing. You may wish to negotiate with the seller

regarding any issues that need to be addressed before you can obtain funding for the purchase.

Amenities
Amenities will add value to the property. The appraiser will note any special features or amenities relevant to the property. You should check this area to ensure that they match your expectations.

Appliances
The inclusion of appliances in the transfer of real estate is not usually a factor related to value from the perspective of the mortgage lender unless the value of the appliances equals a substantial amount of the overall value of a property. You should check this area to ensure that they match your expectations.

Square Feet
The appraiser will enter the total square feet of the property and the number of rooms encompassed by this square footage. He will also note the number of these rooms that are bedrooms and bathroom space.

The appraiser will make adjustments during the valuation processes for the differences in square footage between the property and the comparable property. The appraiser will also make adjustments based on the use of the square footage.

You should check this area to ensure that the entries match your expectations.

Comment
The URAR form provides the appraiser with an area to provide opinion about the property.

This option section has places available to comment on

- Additional features of the property

- Condition of the property including items that presently require repairs, are in a state of deterioration, are undergoing renovations, or have other apparent issues that the appraiser feels may affect the value of the property

- Deficiencies that affect the livability, soundness or structural integrity of the property

- Neighborhood in comparison to the subject property

The appraiser will enter any comments that they feel are important to the ability of the property to maintain its present value. If any item is defined within the comments area that creates a potential for a loss in value, the lender will typically require that the issue be cured, or corrected, before the transaction can proceed to closing. You may wish to negotiate these repairs with the seller. You will also want to review this section to gain a better understanding of what you are purchasing and to ensure that the property meets your expectations.

UNIFORM RESIDENTIAL APPRAISAL REPORT

There are	comparable properties currently offered for sale in the subject neighborhood ranging in price from $		to $	

There are _____ comparable sales in the subject neighborhood within the past twelve months ranging in sales price from $ _____ to $ _____

FEATURE	SUBJECT	COMPARABLE SALE #1	COMPARABLE SALE #2	COMPARABLE SALE #3
Address				
Proximity to Subject				
Sale Price	$	$	$	$
Sale Price/Gross Liv Area	$ sq ft	$ sq ft	$ sq ft	$ sq ft
Data Source(s)				
Verification Source(s)				

VALUE ADJUSTMENTS	DESCRIPTION	DESCRIPTION	Adjustment	DESCRIPTION	Adjustment	DESCRIPTION	Adjustment
Sales or Financing Concessions							
Date of Sale / Time							
Location							
Leasehold/Fee Simple							
Site							
View							
Design (Style)							
Quality of Construction							
Actual Age							
Condition							
Above Grade Room Count	Total / Bdrms / Baths	Total / Bedrms / Baths		Total / Brms / Baths		Total / Brms / Baths	
Gross Living Area	sq ft	sq ft		sq ft		sq ft	
Basement & Finished Rooms Below Grade							
Functional Utility							
Heating / Cooling							
Energy Efficient							
Garage / Carport							
Porch/Patio/Deck							
Net Adjustment		+ -	$	+ -	$	+ -	$
Adjusted Sales Price of Comps		Net Adj % Gross Adj %	$	Net Adj % Gross Adj %	$	Net Adj % Gross Adj %	$

I ___ did ___ did not research the sale or transfer history of the subject property and comparable sales. If not, explain

_____

My research ___ did ___ did not reveal any prior sales or transfers of the subject property for the three years prior to the effective date of this appraisal.
Data source(s) _____

My research ___ did ___ did not reveal any prior sales or transfers of the comparables sales for the year prior to the date of sale of the comparable sale.
Data source(s) _____

Report the results of the research and analysis of the prior sale or transfer history of the subject property and comparable sales (report additional on pg 3)

ITEM	SUBJECT	COMPARABLE SALE #1	COMPARABLE SALE #2	COMPARABLE SALE #3
Date of Prior Sale/Transfer				
Price of Prior Sale/Transfer				
Data Source(s)				
Effective Date of Data Source(s)				

Analysis of prior sale or transfer history of the subject property and comparable sales

_____

Summary of Sales Comparison Approach

_____

Indicated Value by Sales Comparison Approach $ _____

Indicated Value by: Sales Comparison Approach $ _____   Cost Approach (if developed) $ _____   Income Approach (if developed)$ _____

8:8 Sample Form - URAR – Uniform Residential Appraisal Report – HUD Release

166

FEATURE	SUBJECT	COMPARABLE SALE #1		COMPARABLE SALE #2		COMPARABLE SALE #3
Address						
Proximity to Subject						
Sale Price	$	$		$		$
Sale Price/Gross Liv Area	$ sq ft	$ sq ft		$ sq ft		$ sq ft
Data Source(s)						
Verification Source(s)						
VALUE ADJUSTMENTS	DESCRIPTION	DESCRIPTION	Adjustment	DESCRIPTION	Adjustment	DESCRIPTION
Sales or Financing Concessions						
Date of Sale / Time						
Location						
Leasehold/Fee Simple						
Site						
View						
Design (Style)						
Quality of Construction						
Actual Age						
Condition						
Above Grade Room Count	Total Bdrms Baths	Total Bedrms Baths	Baths	Total Brms Baths	Baths	Total Brms Baths
Gross Living Area	sq ft	sq ft		sq ft		sq ft
Basement & Finished Rooms Below Grade						
Functional Utility						
Heating / Cooling						
Energy Efficient						
Garage / Carport						
Porch/Patio/Deck						
Net Adjustment		+ -	$	+ -	$	+ -
Adjusted Sales Price of Comps		Net Adj Gross Adj	$	Net Adj Gross Adj	$	Net Adj Gross Adj

8:9 Sample Form Extraction - URAR – Uniform Residential Appraisal Report – HUD Release

Page two of the URAR will contain the valuation and cost analysis the appraiser completes when assessing the value of the property. The cost analysis may take two forms either the Cost Approach or the Sales Comparison Approach.

Most appraisers are completed using the sales comparison approach.

The sales comparison data assesses the characteristics and condition of your property as compared to other, similar properties sold within a given time period and in the same area as the property. The property should be

- Similar in design and appeal as the subject property
- Similar in size and condition as the subject property

- Similar in features and amenities as the subject property

- Similar in site design, use, and view as the subject property

- Within a defined distance of the subject property

  Example: Within the same neighborhood

- Sold within a pre-set time limit of the date of the appraiser

If a comparable property included on the appraisal does not meet one of these qualifications, the appraiser will need to explain the reason that the comparable was selected as a data source.

Example: Rural property often exceeds the distance requirement as the mass of land encompassed by rural property often makes it difficult to locate many pieces of sold property within the same neighborhood and within the sales time limit.

Your property will be compared to each of the comparables selected by the appraiser.

Proximity
The distance between the properties being compared effects the value.

The appraiser should locate similar properties sold within a reasonable time that are close in location to your property.

Property values vary greatly from one neighborhood to the next. It is important that property comparisons use properties that are located in similarly valued areas.

Sales Price
The sales price of the comparables is the starting basis that will be used to determine the value of your property.

The factors listed below sales price will increase or decrease the value of the property in comparison with other closed sales in the area.

Any area of your property that is lacking as compared to the comparison properties will result in a decrease to the sales price baseline of the comparable.

Any area of your property that is a positive as compared to the comparison properties will result in an increase to the sales price baseline of the comparable.

Sales Price / Gross Living

A dollar figure will be determined for the cost per square foot of the comparable property.

This figure is determined by dividing the total sales price by the total square foot of each property.

The comparable property sales price will be adjusted based on comparison factors between your property and the comparable property. Each of these adjustment items will result in a change in the price valuation.

Data Sources

The appraiser will note the source from which they obtained each entry included in the appraisal.

Concessions

Any concession relating to the transfer of the comparison property will be included as part of the appraisal. These concessions may alter the transaction through an increase in overall value.

The appraiser will also review the sales agreement relating your property to determine if it contains any negotiations relating to seller or finance concessions.

Date of Sale

A date that is too far removed (past) will need to be addressed.

This is a red flag issue for the lender

The loan guidelines for the loan program being obtained will dictate how far in the past a sale may have occurred and still be considered viable for comparison purposes. All comparison property sales should occur within a reasonable time to ensure the correct market conditions are being addressed in regards to value.

At times, the appraiser may exceed the time limitations set by your lender. This exception could occur for a variety of reasons including a slow market in which very few homes have transferred or a neighborhood that contains an exceptionally high number of long-term residences and few property transfers.

The appraiser should include an explanation regarding any property sale used for comparison purposes that exceeds the sale date requirements.

Location

An assessment of average or above is desired with regard to property location.

Any variance between the property assessment level and the assessment of the comparison property may result in an alteration to value.

Estate Type

The type of estate of the subject property should match your expectations. Most real estate transactions are transferred in full using a fee simple transfer. If you receive less than the full bundle of rights with your purchase, the property value and use that you can make of your property can be affected. You should make certain you understand what rights you are obtaining with the property purchase.

Site Size

The sites should be similar in size. A large difference between the land included with the transfer of your property and a comparable property will need to be addressed.

A variance between the site sizes of the properties will result in an alteration to the value.

Sometimes, a large amount of the value of the property is allocated to the land. This could be a problem in closing your loan. Most program guidelines have specific parameters regarding the percentage of the overall property value allocated to the land and the percentage allocated to improvements, setting very specific limits on the amount of the overall value that may be allocated to the land transferred in the sale.

This issue typically arises in the transfer of rural property.

If the land value of your property is excessive, the lender may reduce the value by the amount allocated to the land that is in excess of the loan program guidelines.

View

The sites should be of similar rating concerning view assessment.

A difference in the assessment of the view level between the properties may result in an alteration in the value of your property.

An assessment that indicates a below average rating of the view of your property will need to be explained by the appraiser and may result in stipulations or value changes by the lender.

Design / Style

The properties should be of similar design and appeal levels. A difference in the design and style of the properties will require an explanation by the appraiser. The appraiser will need to define the reason that they chose a comparable property of a different design or style than the subject.

If your property obtains a below average design and appeal assessment this may be a red flag to the lender. Any item that receives a below average rating may require actions on the part of you or seller to correct the issue, additional stipulations, or an alteration to the value assessed to the property.

You will also want to review this entry to ensure that your property meets your expectations.

Quality of Construction

The properties should be of similar quality. Any difference in the quality levels of the property will need to be explained by the appraiser.

A difference in the quality of construction may result in an alteration in the value allowed by the lender.

An assessment that the subject property is of below average construction quality may result in the lender refusing financing on this property, a stipulation that specific repairs be completed to correct the item that is considered to be below average, a change in the value assessment allowed on the property or another action.

You should review this section carefully since the quality of the construction of your new property will affect you even if it does not ultimately affect your loan. If the quality is extremely poor, you may wish to cancel the transaction or negotiate the repair or upgrade in quality with the seller.

Age of Property
The properties used for comparison purposes should be similar to the age of your property. The age of a property affects its value and the appraiser will need to define the reason that the comparables used as data sources are of a different age basis than the subject property.

Room Count /Square Ft
The room counts and square footage of the properties should be similar.

A difference in the room count between your property and the comparable property will result in a change to the value assessment assigned by the appraiser.

The dollar value per square foot calculations will be completed by the appraiser. These act as a baseline for the other value calculations. A large discrepancy in square footage between your property and the comparison property will alter the value assessed by the appraiser.

Basement
The size and use of the basement of your property and comparable properties should be similar. If the basement of the subject property is finished, the basement area of the comparable properties should also be finished.

A variance between the properties will result in an alteration in value.

You should review this area to ensure that the property meets your expectations.

Functional Utility

The functional utility of all of the properties should be similar. A difference in the functional utility of your from the comparables will require an explanation by the appraiser.

A difference in the functional utility may result in an alteration in the value allowed by underwriting.

An assessment that your property is below average may result in underwriting refusing financing on this property, a stipulation that specific repairs be completed to correct the item that is considered to be below average, a change in the value assessment allowed on the property or another action.

The subject property should obtain an assessment of at least average.

An assessment below average will need to be addressed.

You will wish to review this section carefully to ensure the property meets your expectations whether the entries affect your ability to get the loan or not. You may want to negotiate payment for any noted items with the seller.

Heating / Cooling

The heating and cooling systems of the properties will need to be similar.

A difference between the types or inclusion of heating or cooling systems may result in an alteration in value. The type of heating and cooling systems may not be a red flag depending on the region and the commonality of the various heating and cooling systems in use. The addition or exclusion of a cooling system or the age of the heating and cooling system may be a factor to the lender. You will wish to review this section to ensure that the property meets your expectations.

Energy Efficient

The properties should be of similar levels of energy efficiency.

A large discrepancy in the energy efficiency levels of the properties may result in an alteration in value. The property must obtain a rating of at least average. A rating of below average may need to be addressed before you can obtain the loan.

Some loan program guidelines consider a high level of energy efficiency to be a compensating factor.

You will wish to review this section carefully even if it does not affect your loan you will want to ensure that it does match your expectations.

Garage / Carport

The inclusion of a garage or carport should be similar between all properties. The appraiser will assess a value to the garage or carport. The comparison section of the appraisal should reflect the alteration in value that results from the inclusion or lack of a garage or carport in one of the properties.

Porch / Patio / Deck

The inclusion of a porch, patio, or deck should be similar between all properties. The appraiser will assess a value to the porch, patio, or deck. The comparison section of the appraisal should reflect the alteration in value that results from the inclusion or lack of a porch, patio, or deck in one of the properties.

ITEM	SUBJECT	COMPARABLE SALE #1	COMPARABLE SALE #2	COMPARABLE SALE #3
I ___ did ___ did not research the sale or transfer history of the subject property and comparable sales. If not, explain				
My research ___ did ___ did not reveal any prior sales or transfers of the subject property for the three years prior to the effective date of this appraisal.				
Data source(s)				
My research ___ did ___ did not reveal any prior sales or transfers of the comparables sales for the year prior to the date of sale of the comparable sale.				
Data source(s)				
Report the results of the research and analysis of the prior sale or transfer history of the subject property and comparable sales (report additional on pg 3)				
ITEM	SUBJECT	COMPARABLE SALE #1	COMPARABLE SALE #2	COMPARABLE SALE #3
Date of Prior Sale/Transfer				
Price of Prior Sale/Transfer				
Data Source(s)				
Effective Date of Data Source(s)				
Analysis of prior sale or transfer history of the subject property and comparable sales				
Summary of Sales Comparison Approach				
Indicated Value by Sales Comparison Approach $				

8:10 Sample Form Extraction - URAR – Uniform Residential Appraisal Report – HUD Release

Adjustments and Sales Price

The appraiser will enter details relating to your property and each comparable selected as a data source for the determination of value. The upper portion will contain details relating to the sale or transfer of each property, including the date of the sale or transfer. The date entered into the date field must be within the time term established by the lender. If the sale date of a comparable property exceeds the limitations set by lender that affect your loan.

Net Adjustments
The net adjustments section of the appraisal is the area that the appraiser will use to enter the value calculation factors that will help to determine the final value assessed to your property.

Each item that the appraiser assesses for comparison between the properties will be assigned a value.

Any item that was lacking in your property but present in the comparison property will result in a reduction from the sales price of the comparable.

Any item that was lacking in the comparable but present in your property will result in an increase to the sales price of the comparable.

Adjusted Sales Price
These value adjustments will be added to or subtracted from the sales price of the comparable.

Example: Sales Price   199,900
            Garage   + 1,500
            Adjusted Sales Price   201,400

The total dollar figure resulting from these adjustments is the figure the appraiser believes your property would have sold for if given the same buyer, the same time, and the same conditions as the property he is using for comparison.

This is the comparison approach to property valuation.

Signature

The signature of the appraiser indicates he has completed the appraiser and certifies that the market value of the property has been duly determined per appraiser guidelines.

Analysis and Indicated Value

The appraiser will place the value figure he has obtained through comparison, adjustments, and market research on the appraisal page.

This is the final appraised value of the property.

PAGE 3 - Additional Comments

The third page of the appraisal has space for comments of the appraiser.

Any issue noted in the first pages of the appraisal should be addressed in this area.

You should review all of the comments to ensure that you have located each potential red flag contained within the appraisal.

The better informed you are regarding the condition of your property, the more prepared you will be for opening new negotiations with the seller, loan changes that the lender may implement, and handling your new property after you finalize your purchase.

Indicated Value by: Sales Comparison Approach $	Cost Approach (if developed) $	Income Approach (if developed)$

8:11 Sample Form Extraction - URAR – Uniform Residential Appraisal Report – HUD Release

COST APPROACH TO VALUE

The cost approach is used to determine value based upon the replacement cost of the subject property. The cost approach is not usually used for a mortgage loan.

INCOME APPROACH TO VALUE

The income approach to value will often be used for rental or other income producing property. The income approach uses many of the same data indicators as the core appraisal but adds the factor of income to the final value of the property.

PUD PROJECT INFORMATION

If the transaction is being based upon a Planned Unit Development, the PUD section of the appraisal will play a role in the final value determination of the property. You should review this section for any additional red flags that may become apparent if your transaction involves a PUD.

RIGHT TO RECEIVE A COPY OF THE APPRAISAL

When an appraisal has been conducted as a part of the transaction, you have a right to obtain a copy of the appraisal.

- The appraisal will often be delivered directly to the lender during the course of the loan process.

- The lender should provide instructions to you on how to obtain a copy of the appraisal if you desire one at or before the settlement meeting.

- These instructions must be signed and witnessed during the closing process.

Approval and Interest Rates

Each lender that you might work with will have a variety of loan products available. Each product will come with its own set of rules or guidelines that must be met in order to secure that loan. There are many loan programs available from each lender and a vast array of lenders available through a mortgage brokerage. The more familiar your loan officer is with the loan guidelines of the programs he or she has available the more capable he or she will be at placing you in the appropriate program

Each program will have product matrix available for the loan officer to review. These matrix are a snapshot of the minimum requirements needed to place a loan in a particular approval tier or level.

Your responsibility is to provide the loan officer with your wants and needs. This will allow the loan officer to discount any program whose LTV, CLTV, Minimum Purchase Amount and Interest Rate are not suitable for you. Once they have ruled out the unsuitable programs, they will want to examine the programs that they believe are possible matches with your needs in more detail. This allows them to compare with you what is available and determines which programs to submit for possible approval. This is one of the many reasons it is important for you to interview potential loan officers before committing to a specific office for your home lending needs.

If a potential loan officer is only familiar with one or two programs and places each applicant into those programs, he or she may not be the loan officer for you. You will want a loan officer who is willing to spend the extra time and effort researching a variety of programs for which you may qualify to create the best possible situation for you.

Remember you are paying for more than just the loan officer's ability to fill in application forms and submit them to the underwriting department. You are paying the loan officer to be a lending specialist, able and willing to work with you to reach all of your financial goals.

Once a program has been chosen, the loan officer will need to price the loan based on the current rate sheet for that particular program. In the sub-prime industry, rates tend to change more slowly than in the prime market. In some instances, the rate cannot be locked on a sub-prime loan until all conditions have been satisfied. You will want to ask your loan officer exactly how rate locks are handled with your chosen loan program.

The loan officer will compare the specifics of your profile with the requirements of the loan products that they have available. They will usually have a product matrix that shows the guidelines for each requirement.

SAMLE PRODUCT MATRIX

Credit Grade	Credit Score	Mortgage History	Consumer History	Bankruptcy/ Foreclosure	Maximum Debt Ratio	Maximum LTV	Maximum CLTV
A	660+	0x30	1x30	3/3	41%	97%	97%
A-	620-669	1x30	2x30	3/3	45%	95%	97%
B	590-619	2x30	1x60	2/2	47%	90%	95%
B-	560-589	1x60	2x60	2/2	50%	85%	95%
C	540-559	2x60	1x90	1/1	50%	80%	90%
C-	520-539	1x90	2x90	1/1	55%	75%	90%
D	490-519	2x90	3x90	>1year	55%	70%	85%
Contact U/W	>490	>2x90	>3x90	>1 year	55%	Contact U/W	Contact UW

9:1 Sample Loan Product Matrix

Matrix Limitations/Key

- The loan officer will rate your maximum mortgage and consumer late payments against the product matrix. The loan officer will usually use the worst piece of information within your credit profile for rating.

- Each loan program will have a term of credit history that they will review. This history term usually ranges between 12 and 24 months.

- Some matrix will review each piece of history while others will rate you based on credit scores.

- Foreclosure and Bankruptcy dates indicate the date of completion or discharge.

- The loan officer will review your debt to income to determine if you can afford the new housing expense being considered. Some loan matrix will allow higher debt ratios in exchange for a higher interest rate or down payment.

- If you have collection accounts in your credit profile, the loan officer will try to find a program that will work with these collection accounts. Some programs will not allow you to have any collection accounts within your history even if they have been paid in full. Other programs will provide you with an approval as long as all collection accounts are paid prior to closing. Still other programs may allow some collection accounts to remain open. If you have collection accounts within your credit history, you will want to work with your loan officer to find the program that best meets your down payment, pay off allowance and interest rate needs.

- The loan officer will also need to consider the number of credit accounts you have showing in your history. Some lenders require you to have a minimum number of credit accounts showing a clean credit history for a minimum period of time. A common guideline is no fewer than 3 active credit accounts that have been open at least 2 years.

This matrix is for example purposes only. Each loan program will have specific guidelines and approval levels. The loan officer will compare all of your specific information to the guidelines of the loan that they have available. They will determine what level approval you are qualified to receive. This is the loan that you will be offered.

Example:

B	590-619	2x30	1x60	2/2	47%	90%	95%

Based on the example matrix:

A B level borrower will have credit scores between 590 and 619 points.

They will not have been more than 30 days late on their mortgage once in the prior 2 years and 60 days late on a consumer debt once in the last 2 years.

If they have a bankruptcy or foreclosure in their history, it will have been discharged or completed at least 2 years from the date of the application.

They will have debt ratios of less than 47%.

These borrowers would be offered a loan amount at 90% of the sales price of the property.

These borrowers would be allowed to obtain an additional 5% of the sales price of the property in the form of a second loan from either the seller or another lender.

These borrowers would need to provide at least 5% of the sales price of the property as a down payment toward the purchase.

SAMPLE RATE SHEET

Grade	LTV	3/1 ARM			Margin	30 Year Fixed			15 Year Fixed		
		Par	<1.00>	<2.00>		Par	<1.00>	<2.00>	Par	<1.00>	<2.00>
A	97%	8.000	8.500	9.000	4.125	8.500	9.000	9.500	8.000	8.500	9.000
660+	95%	7.875	8.375	8.875	3.875	8.125	8.625	9.125	7.875	8.375	8.875
Mtg 0X30	90%	7.625	8.125	8.625	3.375	8.000	8.500	9.000	7.625	8.125	8.625
Con 1X30	85%	7.250	7.875	8.375	3.250	7.875	8.125	8.625	7.375	7.875	8.375
3/3	80%	7.000	7.500	8.000	3.125	7.750	8.250	8.750	7.000	7.500	8.000
41%	75%	6.750	7.250	7.775	3.000	7.625	8.125	8.625	6.750	7.250	7.775
A-	95%	8.500	9.000	9.500	3.875	9.750	10.250	10.750	8.500	9.000	9.500
620-669	90%	8.125	8.625	9.125	3.375	9.500	10.000	10.500	8.125	8.625	9.125
Mtg 1X30	85%	8.000	8.500	9.000	3.250	9.125	9.625	10.125	8.000	8.500	9.000
Con 2X30	80%	7.875	8.125	8.625	3.125	8.875	9.375	9.875	7.875	8.125	8.625
3/3	75%	7.750	8.250	8.750	3.000	8.375	8.875	9.375	7.750	8.250	8.750
45%	70%	7.625	8.125	8.625	2.875				7.625	8.125	8.625
B	90%	9.750	10.250	10.750	4.125	10.250	10.750	11.250	9.750	10.250	10.750
590-619	85%	9.500	10.000	10.500	3.875	9.625	10.125	10.625	9.500	10.000	10.500
Mtg 2X30	80%	9.125	9.625	10.125	3.375	9.375	9.875	10.375	9.125	9.625	10.125
Con 1X60	75%	8.875	9.375	9.875	3.250	9.250	9.750	10.250	8.875	9.375	9.875
2/2 47%	70%	8.375	8.875	9.375	3.125	8.875	9.250	9.750	8.375	8.875	9.375
B-	85%	10.250	10.750	11.250	5.250	10.875	11.375	11.875	10.250	10.750	11.250
560-589	80%	9.625	10.125	10.625	5.125	10.250	10.750	11.250	9.625	10.125	10.625
Mtg 1X60	75%	9.375	9.875	10.375	5.000	9.625	10.125	10.625	9.375	9.875	10.375
Con 2X60	70%	9.250	9.750	10.250	4.875	9.375	9.875	10.375	9.250	9.750	10.250
2/2 50%											
C	80%	10.875	11.375	11.875	6.250	11.625	12.125	13.125	10.875	11.375	11.875
540-559	75%	10.250	10.750	11.250	6.000	10.875	11.375	12.375	10.250	10.750	11.250
Mtg 2X60	70%	9.625	10.125	10.625	5.875	10.250	10.750	11.750	9.625	10.125	10.625
Con 1X90	65%	9.375	9.875	10.375	5.625	9.750	10.125	11.250	9.375	9.875	10.375
1/1 50%											
C-	75%	11.625	12.125	13.125	7.500	12.375	12.875	13.250	11.625	12.125	13.125
520-539	70%	10.875	11.375	12.375	6.875	11.750	12.250	12.750	10.875	11.375	12.375
Mtg 1X90	65%	10.250	10.750	11.750	6.250	11.125	11.625	12.125	10.250	10.750	11.750
Con 2X90											
1/1 55%											
D	70%	12.375	12.875	13.250	7.875	12.875	13.250	13.875	12.375	12.875	13.250
490-519	65%	11.750	12.250	12.750	7.325	12.250	12.750	13.125	11.750	12.250	12.750
Mtg 2X90											
Con 2X90											
>1 Year 55%											

Pricing assumes 3-year prepayment penalty.
Add .250 to rate for 1-year prepayment penalty.
Add .500 to rate for 0-year prepayment penalty.
No prepayment penalty may be charged on loans >50K.
Loans under 30K require a .500 rate adjustment.

9:2 Sample Loan Rate Sheet

After your loan officer has chosen a program for submittal, they will price the loan based on the current rate sheet for that particular program.

Before your loan officer can begin pricing your loan or determining the interest rate that you will be offered, they will need to make some decisions concerning your loan package. These decisions are based on the information about your situation that the loan officer has gained in your interviews to date. They include:

Your qualifying level
LTV required by you
CLTV required by you
ARM or Fixed loan program
Prepayment penalty option
How the loan officer is being paid – up front fees or wrapped points

To determine your approval level the loan officer will want to refer to your credit report. They will also need to verify the DTI Ratios to be certain they fall within the guidelines of the loan program. The sample rate sheet included is a sub-prime rate sheet. We have used this sample because it better illustrates all of the factors that contribute to a final rate quote. Prime interest rates are calculated and quoted in a similar manner.

You will note that each level has different LTV options. In general, the lower the LTV as compared to the maximum allowed the lower the interest rate. In addition, the higher the credit-grade status the better interest rate you can expect. Keep in mind that using the maximum available options for your Credit Grade will typically increase the interest rate. In this case, the product matrix information has been combined on the rate sheet allowing you to double-check your credit history against the Credit Grade you believe you would qualify for under the matrix guidelines.

The options of Adjustable Rate Mortgage vs. Fixed Rate programs and the use of Prepayment Penalties are explained on the following pages.

The last item that must be decided prior to pricing the loan is how the loan officer will be paid for your loan. When reviewing the Good Faith Estimate you were shown how points are charged on the loan up front. You were also instructed that there was a second method of paying points in the interest rate. This method is called wrapping the points.

These points are passed to you in the form of a higher interest rate. You pay this rate to the lender in monthly increments. The lender, in turn, pays the loan officer for the higher interest rate up front.

Fixed Rate Program

A fixed rate program will often be used if you plan to retain your home or investment property for a longer period than the national average of 3-5 years.

A fixed rate program will be used for a long-term purchaser.

A fixed rate program will often carry a higher interest rate, but will stay stable throughout the life of the loan.

Adjustable Rate Program

An adjustable rate mortgage program (called an ARM) can be customized around your property term, ownership plans, or the market prediction of rate activity.

In many cases, the adjustable rate programs will offer a substantial rate discount to you from the basic fixed rate programs.

Many adjustable rate programs offer 2, 3 even 5-year fixed rates prior to the first adjustment. This encompasses the period that the national average suggests most homeowners will remain in a particular home mortgage. If you are aware of the possibility of a future move, you may benefit from choosing an adjustable rate option. Always research to determine if the rate adjustment is set to occur around the time or after the time, you plan to relocate or sell off the property.

Sometimes, you will want to include a pre-payment penalty in your loan to help lower the interest rate even further.

What is a prepayment penalty?

A prepayment penalty is a monetary penalty that is assessed for the early payoff of a loan containing a prepay clause. Most lenders offer 0, 2, 3, and 5-year prepayment penalties.

These penalties offer the lender security that you will retain the loan for a certain period thereby securing the expected interest payments for the lender. In case of an early payoff, the penalty is designed to offset the loss of interest suffered by the lender.

Lenders will offer a reduction of initial interest rate in exchange for the prepayment clause because of the added longevity of loans on the books.

RATE SHEET KEY

Credit Grade	Your loan officer will rank your credit grade based on a review of your credit report and debt ratios.	Each program will have a different set of terminology for their credit grades. Many will put the basic minimum requirements for each grade level on the rate sheet so the loan officer can double-check the credit history as they price the loan.
Credit Score	Your credit score must be applicable for the program and meet the minimum requirements for the grade level that is being priced.	Keep in mind that different lender's use a different score. Some use the middle credit score ranked by numbers and some will use the most regionally accurate score for your location.

Mortgage History	Each credit grade on the rate sheet included lists the number and the time allowed for that grade mortgage lates in the last 12 months.	If the mortgage history is not on the credit report, you will need to provide documentation proving the mortgage or rental history status over the prior 12-month period.
BK/FC	All credit grades require that a bankruptcy or foreclosure be 'seasoned" for a period of time. This refers to the date of discharge.	If the date is not apparent on the credit report, you will need to provide documentation proving the discharge date.
Consumer Credit	As with Mortgage History, most Credit Grades will require the consumer history meet certain minimum standards.	
Debt Ratio	This rate sheet provides you with the maximum debt ratio allowed under that grade. If your debt load exceeds this ratio, you will be dropped to the nearest grade whose minimum requirements you meet.	Bear in mind that the Debt Ratios must include the new housing payment and any subordinate financing payments you plan to incur because of the purchase.

Also, bear in mind that the Underwriting Team will typically pull another credit report just prior to closing.

Any additional debt you incur between these credit reports will be factored into the debt ratio.

Do not to make credit purchases after application even if the credit is available to you. |

LTV (Loan To Value)	This section lists the maximum loan to value options available for each credit grade.	You will note that there are listings below the maximum LTV available.

In most cases, the lower the actual LTV as compared to the maximum LTV allowed the lower the interest rate offered. |
| ARM/FIXED | The next three columns show the program options.

On this particular rate sheet you have the option of a 2/28 ARM, a 3/1 ARM or a 30 Year Fixed Rate. | Each loan option carries a different interest rate determination.

If you priced at par the rate varies up to 1% between the 2/28 ARM and the 30 Year Fixed Rate |
| PAR | Directly below the term option, you will see PAR, <1.00>, <2.00> <3.00>

To price at par means that there are not points included in the interest rate and your loan officer must obtain their commission points in the good faith estimate and on the HUD Settlement Statement. | To price at <1.00> means that the loan officer/ lending office is receiving 1% of the loan amount as back end commission.

<2.00> means 2% commission points

<3.00> means 3% of the loan amount as back end commission.

This is known as wrapping points or being paid on the back-end. |
| Margin | Beside the Par section, you will see the word Margin.

This only appears on the ARM options.

The margin refers to the rate | The margin is the prime interest rate plus whatever margin is allocated to that program.

For example, on this rate sheet under 3/1 ARM you |

	of adjustment that may occur after the fixed portion of the loan program expires.	will see the margin adjustment is 6.2.
Pricing	Your loan officer will now incorporate all of your options to arrive at an interest rate quote. First, they will find the correct credit grade. They will locate your required loan to value and then follow the column over to the correct loan term option and pricing (back end points). The rate shown is the interest rate you will receive.	Keep in mind that the rate is not locked until you complete the rate lock form.

9:3 Pricing Key

Often a rate sheet will have a variables box somewhere on the page. That variable box allows the rate to be altered by choosing additional options. For instance, if you chose a 5-year prepayment penalty you would be able to reduce the rate quote by .250. If you chose no prepayment penalty, you might be required to increase the rate quote by .750. These variables are very important to the overall rate you will receive.

Chapter

10

THE LOAN PROCESS

We have focused primarily on the lender and loan officer tasks and activities included in the purchase process but the reality is there are a myriad of service providers who must fulfill certain functions in order for you to finalize your loan and close on your new home.

Affinity Group Process

Following the initial application, the loan officer will submit the loan application and all available documentation to the underwriter. The underwriter will review the information submitted and make sure that it conforms to the guidelines of the specific loan program you want. The underwriter will review all of the following aspects of the file:

- Income and Debt Ratios

- Employment History

- Credit History

- Savings / Source of Money for Down Payment

- Appraisal (if available)

Once the underwriter has reviewed the entire file, they will issue a written decision. This may be one of the following:

- Approved - everything is file meets the guidelines for final approval

- Conditional - additional documentation is needed to issue final approval

- Denied - aspects of the file do not conform to the guidelines

This written decision may come with a request for any additional documents that may be needed to complete your loan. These items are called "Conditions". A loan may be approved but still require updated "conditions" or items.

There are two types of conditions:

- Prior to Loan Documents - These items must be provided and reviewed by the underwriter before the loan documents can be requested.

- Prior to Closing - These items must be provided and reviewed by the underwriter or loan funder before the loan can close.

The loan processing of your file is the most time consuming aspect of the loan process. This is the preparation of your file for presentation to the underwriting department. All documentation must be reviewed to insure there are no discrepancies in presentation and any possible issues are worked on at this stage.

If, at the initial application you did not provide all of the original documents that the loan officer asked for, this is the stage where they will be requested again. The loan processing stage may be completed before the loan is submitted to underwriting for review or the package may be sent and then processed based on the stipulation or condition list sent by the underwriter.

The processing stage is comprised of gathering all of the following documents.

- **Verifications of Employment** form sent to past and present employers for the last two years to verify income and time on the job (some employers have an automated 900 # for employment verification). The return of this information usually takes 1-2 weeks.

- **Verifications of Deposit** forms sent to banking institutions to verify average bank account balances for past 3 months (some banks will charge you a fee of up to $20 for this verification). The return of this information usually takes 1-3 weeks.

- **Credit Report** will always be pulled but the loan guidelines may require a full factual credit report, which is the three major credit report bureaus blended onto a single report, with all accounts and balances verified. The verification of accounts usually takes 2-5 days.

- **Escrow Instructions** are drawn up by the Escrow or Closing Company defining the transaction details. Escrow or Closing Companies are independent third parties of the transaction that act as the accountant in the transaction. Some states use closing attorney's or title companies instead of escrow or closing offices. The creation of closing instructions usually takes 2-7 days.

- **Preliminary Title Reports** come from the Title Company who will insure the title of the home. They research the property, the seller, and you for any legal items, liens, or loans that may affect title to the property. The completion of a title search usually takes 1-2 weeks.

- **Appraisals** will be ordered from an underwriting approved appraiser. The appraiser will go to the property, measure square footage, verify required conditions, check other recent comparable home sales, and determine value of the home. Appraisals usually take 1-4 weeks to complete.

- **Purchase Contract, Counter Offers, and Transfer Disclosure Statements** are required for purchase transactions only. These are the original contracts regarding the terms of the purchase of your property. All of the completed and signed documents will be needed prior to ordering the appraisal. The realtors will typically provide the finalized sales contract and any addendums to your loan officer. Negotiation of the sales contract usually takes 2-10 days.

- **Letters of Explanation** are letters written and signed by you to explain any issues on the credit report, work history, bank account deposits, source of funds, etc. These letters are usually completed after receipt of all other documents necessary for the loan.

- **Additional supporting documents** may be needed on a case-by-case scenario, such as 12 months cancelled checks to verify making payments or receiving income, complete bankruptcy, divorce, child support papers. This will vary by your individual scenario. The amount of time necessary to obtain these documents really depends on you.

- **Any Documents missing from initial loan application** such as 2 months recent pay stubs, 3 months complete bank statements, or last 2 years tax returns will be needed before the processing stage is complete. The amount of time necessary to obtain these documents really depends on you.

Since all of these documents are secured from various companies and individuals, the loan processing stage is most the most common place for delays in your process.

Once the Underwriting department has satisfied all stipulations, your closing will be scheduled and the closing documents will be requested from the lenders closing department.

The loan document process is the stage when the funding agent is preparing the loan documents. These loan documents are the legal binding documents that you must sign to finalize the transaction.

Finalize Conditions
Once all of the conditions listed on the stipulation list have been cleared, the loan officer or loan processor will submit the package to underwriting for a final review and approval.

Pre-Close
Once underwriting has issued the final loan commitment and the closing is scheduled, your loan officer or loan processor should contact you to perform a pre-close discussion.

They will review the final terms of the loan with you and if you have not locked the interest rate prior to this time, the loan officer will prepare a lock request for you to submit.

The loan officer should review your loan terms with you to ensure that you understand everything about the new loan you are receiving.

Closing

The closing company will schedule the closing. You are required to attend the closing and to sign all of the documents presented to you as part of obtaining your new mortgage loan.

A closing agent will conduct the settlement, presenting each document to you for review and signing. Your loan officer, real estate agent, the seller or another party might attend the closing with you.

They will include some of the following important items to be signed at the closing.

Note – You will sign a Promissory Note indicating the amount borrowed, the interest rate charged, and the terms or repayment of the loan including the monthly payment amount.

Deed of Trust – You will sign a deed of trust that places the property as security to the loan and note. This will be recorded with the county recorders office.

HUD 1 – You will review and sign the HUD 1 Settlement Statement that breaks down all fees incurred for obtaining the loan.

The lender will typically also require that you complete additional legal forms to help confirm that you understand the transaction, to verify your statements during the loan process, and to promote the security for the lender of the transaction.

Occupancy Declaration

An occupancy declaration is a statement by you that defines the use you intend to make of the property.

When a mortgage lender provides a mortgage loan, one aspect that will affect the approval is the use that you intend to make of the property.

It is commonly believed that a borrower will make payments against their primary residence better than they will against a second home, investment property or other form of residence. As such, the entry that you make on the application form pertaining to occupancy plans of the property will change many aspects of the loan including interest rate, loan to value and documentation requirements among others.

It is a common practice to request that you complete a statement that confirms these occupancy plans during the settlement meeting.

A closing could be stopped if you refuse to sign an occupancy declaration.

MAILING ADDRESS CONFIRMATION / PAYMENT LETTER

From:

Re: Loan #   *** IMPORTANT, PLEASE READ THROUGHOULY ***

            Property Address

To:

Dear Homeowner:

A.   All mortgage servicing correspondence will be mailed to the above referenced property address. In order to ensure proper receipt of all mortgage servicing notifications (i.e. monthly statement, Q&A booklets, etc.)

please   indicate the correct mailing address if it is different from the property address. The address to mail payments

and   the phone number to call for customer service are listed below.

      Please indicate (X):

      ( )   The property address is correct as referenced above and should be used for correspondence.

      ( )   The proper mailing address is: _____

B.   The monthly payments on the above loan are to begin on   , and will continue monthly until

      Your monthly payment will consist of the following:

      MONTHLY PAYMENT ………………………………………….$ _____

      MMI/PMI INSRUANCE ………………………………………….. _____

      RESERVE FOR COUNTY TAXES ………………………………… _____

      RESERVE FOR HAXARD INSURANCE……………………………. _____

      RESERVE FOR FLOOD INSURANCE…………………………….. _____

      RESERVE FOR CITY TAXES……………………………………._____

      RESERVE FOR ANNUAL ASSESSMENT……………………………._____

      RESERVE FOR SCHOOL TAXES…………………………………….._____

      _____...................................._____

                 TOTAL MONTHLY PAYMENTS………$_____

*** Please be aware that if you have an impound account, you may see a change in your initial monthly payment figure due to information available after the closing of your loan.

Engages the services of   as its servicer. You will be receiving a billing notice from   within two weeks of your loan funding.   has the right to collect your payments and this in no way affects the terms and conditions of the mortgage instruments, other than the terms directly related to the servicing of your loan. If you do not receive a payment booklet or have other questions about the servicing of your loan, please call:

Please send your payments to:

Any correspondences, or calls, in reference to your loan, please refer to the above loan number. However, your loan number will be changed for servicing purposes.

Copy received and acknowledged.

11:1 Sample Form – Occupancy Declaration and Address Confirmation – HUD Release

Fee Disclosure

Many lenders now require that you give them payment for certain fees during the loan process. These funds are held by the lender to pay for services that will be ordered in relationship to documenting the loan.

Other fees may be paid directly to service providers during the transaction processing stage or paid out of the proceeds at the closing table.

The lender will provide you with a fee disclosure to sign before or at the settlement.

FEE DISCLOSURE	
APPLICANT(S) NAME AND ADDRESS	MORTGAGE BANKER/BROKER NAME AND ADDRESS
PROPERTY ADDRESS	TYPE OF LOAN

Today you have submitted a mortgage loan application to the Mortgage Banker or Broker listed above. All fees paid by you are nonrefundable. State law (   ) requires that the following information be disclosed to you.

The Mortgage Banker or Broker is required to refund all fees paid by an applicant borrower, other than those fees paid by the Mortgage Banker or Broker to a third party, when a mortgage loan is not produced within the time specified by the Mortgage Banker or Broker at the rate, term and overall cost agreed to by the borrower.

However, this provision shall not apply when the failure to produce a loan is due solely to the borrower's negligence, borrower's refusal to accept and close on a loan commitment or borrower's refusal or inability to provide information necessary for processing the loan, including, but not limited to, employment verifications and verifications of deposit.

This disclosure does not constitute approval of your loan or a commitment to make a loan to you.

11:1 Sample Form – Fee Disclosure – HUD Release

Funding

Funding is the time when all of your signed documents are reviewed by the lender to insure that everything is completed correctly.

At this point, the lender will also do a final back-up quality control check of your credit and employment to insure nothing has changed since the loan was approved.

Once everything has been verified and checked, the lender will fund the loan.

The funding of the loan is the time when the monies that you have borrowed are wired to the closing company, escrow office, or the closing attorney for disbursement.

This is when the actual exchange of money is completed.

This funding is usually completed through an electronic wire transfer.

Some lenders do dry closings in which the funds are not sent until all the review activity is complete.

In this case, the funding will usually take place 2 to 4 days after the loan documents have been returned to the lender by the closer.

In other cases, lenders send the funds to the escrow or closing company before the settlement meeting. If the funds are available at the settlement meeting, the escrow or closing agent will cut the checks and have them available for dispersal at the settlement table.

Recording

The recording process is the time that the legal, binding loan documents that you signed are taken to the county recorder office for recording.

The actual recording is simply the time when the documents are time and date stamped by the county recorder office, recognized, and filed as an official public document.

The recording process usually takes place 24 to 48 hours after the loan has been funded and the electronic wire confirmed.

In some places a "special recording" or a same day recording may occur.

At this point, your loan is finalized and closed and you are a new homeowner.

You can take the keys from the closing meeting and move into the new home that you have worked so hard to attain.

Congratulations on completing the process of gaining the knowledge and tools that you need to obtain the right mortgage loan to meet the needs of you and your family. The process of finding a home, making an acceptable offer and getting the funds you need to complete the process can be a long and complex one. By ensuring that you are well educated about every step of the process, you have made a huge contribution toward protecting yourself, your family, and your finances over the coming years.

Congratulations and welcome home!

Appendix

GLOSSARY OF MORTGAGE TERMS

1-year ARM: An adjustable-rate mortgage (ARM) that has an initial interest rate for one year, and thereafter has an adjustment interval of one year. The adjustment is based on comparison interest caps and the indexed rate

3/1 ARM: An adjustable-rate mortgage (ARM) that has an initial interest rate for three years, and thereafter has an adjustment interval of one year. The adjustment is based on comparison interest caps and the indexed rate.

5/1 ARM: An adjustable-rate mortgage (ARM) that has an initial interest rate for five years, and thereafter has an adjustment interval of one year. The adjustment is based on comparison interest caps and the indexed rate

7/1 ARM: An adjustable-rate mortgage (ARM) that has an initial interest rate for seven years, and thereafter has an adjustment interval of one year. The adjustment is based on comparison interest caps and the indexed rate

10/1 ARM: An adjustable-rate mortgage (ARM) that has an initial interest rate for ten years, and thereafter has an adjustment interval of one year. The adjustment is based on comparison interest caps and the indexed rate

Abstract of Title: A written history of all the transactions that bear on the title to a specific piece of land. An abstract of title covers the time from when the property was first sold to the present. Used by the Title Company to produce a title binder

Acceleration Clause: The section of a mortgage document that allows the lender to speed up the payment date in the event of default, making the entire principal amount due

Acre: An area of land 43.560 square feet

Adjustable Rate Mortgage: Mortgage in which the rate of interest is adjusted based on a standard

rate index. Most ARM's have caps on how much the interest rate may increase

Adjustment Interval: How often the loan's rate can be changed

Alternative Mortgage: 7/23 and 5/25 mortgages with a one-time rate adjustment after seven years and five years respectively. Also known as a hybrid mortgage or a two-step mortgage

Amortization Schedule : A timetable for the gradual repayment of a mortgage loan. An amortization schedule indicates the amount of each payment applied to interest and principal, and the remaining balance after each payment is made

Amortization Term: The amount of time required to amortize (repay) a mortgage loan. The amortization term is usually expressed in months. A 30-year fixed rate mortgage, for example, has an amortization term of 360 months

Annual Percentage Rate (APR): A standardized method of calculating the cost of a mortgage, stated as a yearly rate which includes such items as interest, mortgage insurance, and certain points or credit costs

Appraisal: A written report by a qualified appraiser estimating the value of the property

Appraised Value: An opinion of a property's fair market value, based on an appraiser's inspection and analysis of the property

Appraiser: A person qualified by education, training, and experience to estimate the value of real property

Appreciation: An increase in the value of a property due to changes in market conditions or improvements to the property

ARM: See Adjustable Rate Mortgage

Assessed Value: The value of a property as determined by a public tax assessor for the purpose of taxation

Assumable: A mortgage that a buyer can assume, or take over, from the seller of the property

Balloon Mortgage: A loan that has regular monthly payments, which amortize over a stated term but call for a final lump sum (balloon payment) at the end of a specified term, or maturity date such as 10 years

Basis Points: 1/100th of 1 percent If an interest rate changes 50 basis points, for example, it has move ½ of 1 percent

Binder: See title binder

Biweekly Mortgage: A mortgage that schedules payments every two weeks instead of the standard monthly payment. The 26 biweekly payments are each equal to one-half of the monthly payment. The result for the borrower is a substantial reduction in interest payments because the mortgage is paid off sooner. See also prepayment plan

Bridge loan: A loan that "bridges" the gap between the purchase of a new home and the sale of the borrower's current home. The borrower's current home is used as collateral and the money is used to close on the new home before the current home is sold. Some are structured so they completely pay off the old home's first mortgage at the bridge loan's closing. Others pile the new debt on top of the old. They usually run for a term of six months

Broker: See mortgage broker

Broker Premium: A premium paid to the mortgage broker as the "middleman" in the mortgage process between the lender and the borrower

Built-ins: Cabinets, ranges, ceiling fans and other items permanently attached to the structure, and which a buyer may assume will remain with the structure

Buy down: The process of trading money for a lower mortgage rate. The borrower "buys down" the interest rate on a mortgage by paying discount points up front. It can also be a mortgage in which an initial lump sum payment is made to reduce a borrower's monthly payments during the first few years of a mortgage

Caps: The maximum amount the interest rate can change annually or cumulatively over the life of an adjustable rate mortgage. F or example, if the caps are 2 percent annual and 6 percent life of loan, a mortgage with a first-year rate of 10 percent could rise to no more than 12 percent the second year, and no more than 16 percent over the entire life of the loan

Certificate of Title: A statement provided by the Title Company or attorney stating that the title to the real estate is legally held by the current owner

Chattel: Personal property

Clear title: A title that is free of liens or legal questions as to ownership of a piece of property

Closing: The meeting at which the sale of a property is finalized The buyer signs the lender agreement for the mortgage and pays' closing costs and escrow amounts. The buyer and seller sign documents to transfer the ownership of the property. Also known as the settlement

Closing costs: Expenses incurred by buyers and sellers in transferring ownership of a property. Closing costs normally include an origination fee, an attorney's fee, taxes, escrow payments, and charges for title insurance. Lenders or Real Estate Agents provide estimates of closing costs to prospective homebuyers

Closing Statement: A financial disclosure accounting for all funds changing hands at the closing See also HUD-1 Statement

Cloud on title: Any fact or condition that could adversely affect the title

Commission: In real estate, the broker, or mortgage associates fee for assisting in the transaction. Usually expressed as a percentage of the total paid by the buyer

Commitment: A formal offer by a lender stating the approved terms for lending money to a homebuyer

Common Area Assessment: A levy against individual unit owners in a condominium or planned unit development to pay for upkeep, repairs, and improvements to the property's common areas, such as corridors, elevators, parking lots, swimming pools and tennis courts

Comparables: Refers to "comparable properties" which are used for comparative purposes in the appraisal process. Comps are recently sold properties that are similar in size, location, and amenities to the home for sale. Comps help an appraiser determine the fair market value of a property

Condominium: A real estate project in which each unit owner has title to a unit of the project, and sometimes and undivided interest in the common areas

Conforming Loan: A loan that conforms to the standard rules for purchase by Freddie Mac or Fannie Mae

Contingency: A condition that must be met before a contract is legally binding. For example, homebuyers often include a contingency that specifies that the contract is not binding until after a satisfactory report from a home inspector

Contract: In real estate parlance, the contract is the legal document by which buyer and seller make offers and counteroffers. The real estate contract describes the property, includes or excludes items in the property, names the price, apportions the closing costs between the parties and sets forth a closing date. When a buyer and seller agree on the terms and sign the same document the property is said to be "under contract". More formally known as the agreement for the sale, purchase agreement, or earnest money contract

Conventional Mortgage: Usually refers to a fixed-rate, 30-year mortgage that is not insured by FHA, Farmers Home Administration, or Veterans Administration

Convertible Mortgage: An adjustable rate mortgage ARM that can be converted to a fixed mortgage under specific conditions

Cooperative: A type of multiple ownership in which the residents of a multiunit housing complex own shares in the cooperative corporation that owns the property, giving each resident the right to occupy a specific apartment or unit

Cost-of-funds: A yield index based upon the cost of funds to savings & loan institution in the San Francisco Federal Home Loan Bank District. It is one of the indexes commonly used to set the rate of adjustable rate mortgages

Covenant: A written restriction on the use of land, most commonly in use today in homeowners associations

Credit report: A report on a person's credit history prepared by a credit bureau and used by a lender in determining a loan applicant's record for paying debts in a timely manner

Debt-to-Income Ratio: The percentage of a person's monthly earnings used to pay off all debt obligations Lenders consider two ratios, constructed in slightly different ways. The first called the front-end ratio, the ratio of the monthly housing expenses – including principal, interest, property taxes, and insurance, (PITI) is compared to the borrower's gross, pretax monthly income. In the back-end ratio, a borrower's other debts such as auto loans and credit cards are figured in.

Lenders usually consider both and set an acceptable ratio. Some lenders and some lending qualifying agencies only consider the back-end ratio

Deed: The legal document conveying title to the property

Depreciation: A decline in the value of a property as opposed to appreciation

Discount Points: A type of point (1 percent of the loan) paid by the borrower to reduce the interest rate

Down payment: The amount of a property's purchase price that the buyer pays in cash and does not finance with a mortgage

Earnest money: A deposit made by potential homebuyers during negotiations with the seller. The sum shows a seller that the buyer is serious about purchasing a property

Easement: The right of another to use a property The most common easements are for utility lines

80-10-10 Loan: A combination of an 80 percent loan-to-value first mortgage, a 10 percent down payment and a 10 percent home equity loan. This is also sometimes referred to as a CLTV (Combined Loan-to-Value)

Encumbrance: A lien, charge, or liability against a property

Equal Credit: A federal law that requires lenders and other creditors to make credit equally available with out discrimination based on race, color, religion, national origin, age, sex, marital status, or receipt of income from public assistance programs

Equity: The value of a homeowner's unencumbered interest in real estate Equity is the difference between the homes fair market value and the unpaid balance of the mortgage and any outstanding liens Equity increases as the mortgage is paid down or as the property enjoys appreciation

Escrow Payment: The portion of a homeowner's monthly mortgage payment that is held by the loan servicer to pay for taxes and insurance Also known as reserves The loan servicer holds the escrow funds separately from money meant to pay principal and interest

Fair Credit Reporting Act: A consumer protection law that regulates the disclosure of consumer credit reports by credit reporting agencies and establishes procedures for correcting mistakes on a person's credit record

Fannie Mae: Nickname for Federal National Mortgage Association It is a government-chartered non-bank financial services company and the nation's largest source of financing for home mortgages It was started to make sure mortgage money is available in all areas of the country

FHA Mortgage: A mortgage insured by the Federal Housing Administration

First mortgage: A mortgage that is the primary lien against a property

Fixed-rate Mortgage: A mortgage in which the interest rate does not change during the entire term of the loan, most often 15, or 30 years

Flood Insurance Insurance that compensates for the physical property damage resulting from rising water It is required for properties located in federally designated flood areas

Foreclosure: The legal process by which a homeowner in default on a mortgage is deprived of interest in the property This usually involves a forced sale of the property at public auction with the proceeds of the sale being applied to the mortgage debt

Freddie Mac: Nickname for Federal Home Loan Mortgage Corp A financial corporation chartered by the federal government to buy pools of mortgages from lenders and sell securities backed by these mortgages

Ginnie Mae: Nickname for the Government National Mortgage Association

Good Faith Estimate: A written estimate of closing costs that the lender must provide to prospective homebuyers within three days of submitting a mortgage loan application

Government National Mortgage Association (Ginnie Mae) A government-owned corporation within the US Department of Housing and Urban Development (HUD) Created by Congress in 1968, GNMA has responsibility for the special assistance loan program known as Ginnie Mae

Hazard Insurance: Insurance coverage that compensates for physical damage to property from natural disasters such as fire and other hazards Depending on where a piece of property is located, lenders may also require flood

insurance or policies covering windstorms (hurricanes) or earthquakes

Home Inspection: An inspection by a building professional that evaluates the structural and mechanical condition of a property

Homeowners Association: A nonprofit association that manages the common areas of a condominium or PUD Unit owners pay the association a fee to maintain areas owned jointly

Homeowner's Insurance: An insurance policy that combines personal liability insurance and hazard insurance coverage for a residence and its contents

Housing Expense: The percentage of gross monthly income that goes toward paying a Ratio mortgage or rent on a home

HUD-1: The document with an itemized listing of closing costs payable at the closing or settlement meeting when buying property The closing costs can include a commission, loan fees, and points, and sums set aside for escrow payments, taxes, and insurance It is signed by both the buyer and the seller, who may be paying some of the closing costs The statement form is published by HUD

Hybrid Mortgage: See alternative mortgage products.

Index: A published measure of the cost of money that lenders use to calculate the rate on an ARM The most common indexes are the one-year Treasury Constant Maturity Yield and the FHLB 11th District Cost of Funds

Indexed Rate: The sum of the published index plus the margin For example, if the index were 9 percent and the margin 2.75 percent, the indexed rate would be 11.75 percent. Often, lenders charge less than the indexed rate the first year of an ARM

Initial Interest Rate: Starting rate of an ARM

Interest Tax Deduction: Most mortgage holders can deduct all the interest paid on the loan in filing income tax The deduction applies to people with just on mortgage on a primary residence, as well as those with a combination of loans. Within certain time limits set by the IRS, points paid up front on a mortgage are usually deductible in the year the house was purchased

Jumbo Mortgage: Mortgages larger than the limits set by Fannie Mae and Freddie Mac. A jumbo mortgage will carry a higher interest rate than a conventional mortgage

Lease-purchase   A financing option that allows a potential homebuyer to lease a property with the option to buy   Often constructed so the monthly rent payment covers the owner's first mortgage payment, plus an additional amount as a savings deposit to accumulate cash for a down payment A seller may agree to a lease-purchase option if the housing market is saturated and the seller is having a difficult time selling the property

Lien: A legal hold or claim from one person on the property of another   The lien placed by a first mortgage is special. It is called a first lien and takes precedence over others

Lifetime Rate Cap: In an ARM, it limits the amount that the interest rate can increase or decrease over the life of the loan. See also caps

Lis Pendens: A pending lawsuit; in real estate, the constructive notice filed in public records that a legal dispute exists over a piece of property

Livery of Seizen: Under common law, the process of transferring title

Loan Origination: The process by which a mortgage lender obtains a mortgage secured by real property   An origination fee is charged by the lender to process all forms involved in obtaining a mortgage

Loan-to-value (LTV) Ratio: The ratio of a mortgage loan amount to the property's appraised value or selling price, whichever is less   For example, if a home is sold for $100,000 and the mortgage amount is $80,000 the LTV is 80%

Lock: Lender's guarantee that the mortgage rate quoted will be good for a specific amount of time. The homebuyer usually wants the lock to stay in effect until the date of the closing

Lock-and-Float: Rate programs offered by companies that allow borrowers to lock in the current interest rate on a mortgage for a specified period, while also letting them "float" the rate down if market conditions improve before closing

Low-down Mortgages: Mortgages with a low down payment, usually less than 10 percent. Frannie Mae and Freddie Mac design loan programs that spell out a set of standards for lenders. In recent years, these government-chartered agencies have made low-down mortgages more available

Margin: The number of percentage points added to the index on a one-year ARM

Maturity : The date on which the principal balance of a loan becomes due and payable

Mortgage: A legal document that uses property as collateral to secure payment of a debt

Mortgage Banker: The lender that originates a mortgage loan, the one making the loan directly, and closing the loan

Mortgage Broker: An individual or company that brings borrowers and lenders together for the purpose of loan origination   Unlike a mortgage banker, brokers do not fund the loan but work on behalf of several lenders. Brokers typically require a fee or a commission for their service   See broker premium

Mortgage Insurance: A policy that insures the lender against loss should the homeowner default on a mortgage. Depending on the loan, the insurance can be issued by government agencies such as the FHA or a private company. It is part of the monthly mortgage payment. (See also private mortgage insurance PMI)

Negative Amortization: A gradual increase in mortgage debt that happens when a monthly payment does not cover the entire principal and interest due   The shortfall is added to the remaining balance to create "negative" amortization

No-doc or low-doc Loan: These no-documentation or low-documentation loans are designed for the entrepreneur or self-employed, for recent immigrants with money in foreign countries or for borrowers who cannot or choose not to reveal information about their incomes

Note: The document giving evidence of mortgage indebtedness, including the amount and terms of repayment

Origination Fee: A fee paid to the lender for processing a loan application

Owner financing A transaction in which the seller of a house provides all or part of the financing Sellers may provide financing because they need to sell the property right away or they are having difficulty selling the house and want to provide financing as an incentive to a buyer

Periodic rate cap: In an ARM, it limits how much an interest rate can increase or decrease during any one-adjustment period   See also caps

PITI: Stands for principal, interest, taxes and insurance that are the usual components of a monthly mortgage payment

PITI Reserves: A cash amount that a homebuyer must have on hand after making a down payment and paying all closing costs. The reserves required by a lender must equal the amount a buyer would pay for PITI for a specific number of months

Plat: A map that shows a parcel of land and how it is subdivided into individual lots Plat maps also show the locations of streets and easements

PMI: See private mortgage insurance

Points: A point equals 1 percent of a mortgage loan. Lenders charge points as a way to make a profit. Borrowers may pay discount points to reduce the loan interest rate. Buyers are prohibited from paying points on HUD or VA guaranteed loans

Pre-approval: This process goes a step further than pre-qualification. It means the lender has contacted the borrower's employer, bank, and other places to verify all claims of earnings and assets. In return, the borrower receives a letter stating the lender is willing to grant a mortgage for a specific amount within a limited period with the stipulation that there are no material changes to the borrower's situation

Prepayment Penalty: A fee imposed by certain lenders if the first mortgage is paid off early

Prepayment Plan: Similar to biweekly mortgage, but operated by a third party In it, the borrower pays to the third party, half the monthly mortgage payment every two weeks At the end of the year, the plan operators typically take the extra money that results from the process and sends lump sum payment to the participants' lenders

Pre-qualification: An early evaluation by a lender of a potential homebuyer's credit report, plus earnings, savings, and debt information The homebuyer gets a non-binding estimate of the mortgage amount the borrower would qualify for, or how much house the borrower can afford. Buyers who pre-qualify can go a step further and seek a pre-approval

Rate Lock: A commitment issued by a lender to the homebuyer or the mortgage broker guaranteeing a specific interest rate for a specified amount of time See also lock

Real Estate Agent: A person licensed to negotiate and transact the sale of real estate on behalf of the property owner

RESPA: Real Estate Settlement Procedures Act. A consumer protection law that requires lenders to give homebuyers advance notice of closing costs, which are payable at the closing or settlement meeting

Realtor: A real estate broker or an associate who holds an active membership in a local real estate board that is affiliated with the National Association of Realtors

Refinancing: Securing a new loan in order to pay off the existing mortgage or to gain access to the existing equity in the home

Roll-in Loan: A refinance loan that rolls any closing costs or fees into the loan. These programs best serve people who have a reasonable amount of equity, want to reduce their overall interest expense, and plan to stay in their homes

Rural Housing Service (RHS): The agency in the US Department of Agriculture providing financing to farmers and other qualified borrowers buying property in rural areas who are unable to obtain loans elsewhere. It offers low-interest-rate loans with no down payment to borrowers with low-to-moderate incomes who live in rural areas or small towns

Sales Agreement: A written contract signed by the buyer and the seller of a house stating the terms and conditions under which the property will be sold

Second Mortgage: A mortgage on the property that has a lien position behind the first mortgage

Servicer: An organization that collects monthly mortgage principal and interest payments from homeowners and manages escrow accounts for paying taxes and homeowners' insurance premiums The servicer often services mortgages that have been purchased by an investor in the secondary mortgage market

Settlement: See closing

Sub-prime Mortgage: A mortgage granted to a borrower considered sub-prime, that is, a person with a less-than perfect credit report. Sub-prime borrowers either have missed payments on a debt or have been late with payments. Lenders charge a higher interest rate to compensate for potential losses from customers who may run into trouble and default

Time is of the Essence: A phrase inserted in contracts to require a punctual performance

Title: A legal document proving a person's right to claim entitlement to a property, including the history of the property's ownership

Title Binder: Written evidence of temporary title insurance coverage

Title Company: A company that specializes in examining and insuring titles to real estate

Title insurance: Insurance that protects against loss from disputes over ownership of a property. A policy may protect the mortgage lender and/or the homebuyer

Title search: A check of title records to ensure that the seller is the legal owner of a property and that there are no liens or other claims against the property

Transfer Tax: State or local tax levied when title passes from one owner to another

Treasury Index: An index used to determine interest rate changes for certain ARM mortgages.

It is based on the results of auctions that the US Treasury holds for its Treasury bills and securities or is derived from the US Treasury's daily yield curve, which is based on the closing market bid yields on actively traded Treasury securities in the over-the-counter market

Truth-in-Lending Act (TILA): A federal law that requires lenders to disclose, in writing, the terms and conditions of a mortgage, including the annual percentage rate APR and other charges

Underwriter: A company or person undertaking the responsibility for issuing a mortgage. Underwriters analyze a borrower's credit worthiness and set the loan amount

VA Mortgage: A loan backed by the Veterans Administration. It requires very low or no down payments and has less stringent requirements for qualification. Members of the US armed forces are eligible for the loans under certain qualifying conditions

Wraparound Mortgage: A new mortgage that includes the remaining balance on the old mortgage plus a new amount

www.ingramcontent.com/pod-product-compliance
Lightning Source LLC
Chambersburg PA
CBHW051345200326
41521CB00014B/2480